FIRST NAME   SURNAME

HOME ADDRESS (LINE 1)

HOME ADDRESS (LINE 2)

HOME PHONE   MOBILE PHONE

EMAIL

TWITTER   INSTAGRAM

BUSINESS/COLLEGE ADDRESS (LINE 1)

BUSINESS/COLLEGE ADDRESS (LINE 2)

BUSINESS/COLLEGE PHONE   BUSINESS/COLLEGE EMAIL

EMERGENCY CONTACT (NAME AND PHONE NUMBER)

BLOOD GROUP

ALLERGIES

VACCINATIONS

UK BANK HOLIDAYS

JANUARY 2ND — New Year's Day (observed)

APRIL 7TH — Good Friday

APRIL 10TH — Easter Monday

MAY 1ST — Early May Bank Holiday

MAY 29TH — Spring Bank Holiday

AUGUST 28TH — Summer Bank Holiday

DECEMBER 25TH — Christmas Day

DECEMBER 26TH — Boxing Day

US FEDERAL HOLIDAYS

JANUARY 2ND — New Year's Day (observed)

JANUARY 16TH — Martin Luther King Jr. Day

FEBRUARY 20TH — Presidents' Day

MAY 29TH — Memorial Day

JUNE 19TH — Juneteenth

JULY 4TH — Independence Day

SEPTEMBER 4TH — Labor Day

OCTOBER 9TH — Indigenous Peoples' Day

NOVEMBER 10TH — Veterans Day (observed)

NOVEMBER 23RD — Thanksgiving

DECEMBER 25TH — Christmas Day

Verso Books is the largest independent,
radical publishing house in the English-speaking world.

Launched by *New Left Review* in 1970, Verso
is a leading publisher in current affairs, philosophy,
history, politics and economics.

"A rigorously intelligent publisher."
—*SUNDAY TIMES*

"Anglo-America's preeminent radical press."
—*HARPER'S*

VERSOBOOKS.COM

Buy securely and easily from our website—
great discounts, free shipping with a minimum order
and a free ebook bundled with many of our hard-copy books.

Check our website to read our blog and see our
latest titles—featuring essays, videos, podcasts,
interviews with authors, news, exclusive competitions
and details of forthcoming events.

Sign up to our email list to be the first to hear of
our new titles, special offers and events.

Verso Books   @VersoBooks   versobooks

Some of the quotes in the calendar are drawn
from *The Verso Book of Dissent*, edited by
Andrew Hsiao and Audrea Lim (Verso 2020).

2023

JANUARY

S	M	T	W	TH	F	S
1	2	3	4	5	6	7
8	9	10	11	12	13	14
15	16	17	18	19	20	21
22	23	24	25	26	27	28
29	30	31	1	2	3	4

FEBRUARY

S	M	T	W	TH	F	S
29	30	31	1	2	3	4
5	6	7	8	9	10	11
12	13	14	15	16	17	18
19	20	21	22	23	24	25
26	27	28	1	2	3	4

MARCH

S	M	T	W	TH	F	S
26	27	28	1	2	3	4
5	6	7	8	9	10	11
12	13	14	15	16	17	18
19	20	21	22	23	24	25
26	27	28	29	30	31	1

APRIL

S	M	T	W	TH	F	S
26	27	28	29	30	31	1
2	3	4	5	6	7	8
9	10	11	12	13	14	15
16	17	18	19	20	21	22
23	24	25	26	27	28	29
30						

MAY

S	M	T	W	TH	F	S
30	1	2	3	4	5	6
7	8	9	10	11	12	13
14	15	16	17	18	19	20
21	22	23	24	25	26	27
28	29	30	31	1	2	3

JUNE

S	M	T	W	TH	F	S
28	29	30	31	1	2	3
4	5	6	7	8	9	10
11	12	13	14	15	16	17
18	19	20	21	22	23	24
25	26	27	28	29	30	1

JULY

S	M	T	W	TH	F	S
25	26	27	28	29	30	1
2	3	4	5	6	7	8
9	10	11	12	13	14	15
16	17	18	19	20	21	22
23	24	25	26	27	28	29
30	31					

AUGUST

S	M	T	W	TH	F	S
30	31	1	2	3	4	5
6	7	8	9	10	11	12
13	14	15	16	17	18	19
20	21	22	23	24	25	26
27	28	29	30	31	1	2

SEPTEMBER

S	M	T	W	TH	F	S
27	28	29	30	31	1	2
3	4	5	6	7	8	9
10	11	12	13	14	15	16
17	18	19	20	21	22	23
24	25	26	27	28	29	30

OCTOBER

S	M	T	W	TH	F	S
1	2	3	4	5	6	7
8	9	10	11	12	13	14
15	16	17	18	19	20	21
22	23	24	25	26	27	28
29	30	31	1	2	3	4

NOVEMBER

S	M	T	W	TH	F	S
29	30	31	1	2	3	4
5	6	7	8	9	10	11
12	13	14	15	16	17	18
19	20	21	22	23	24	25
26	27	28	29	30	1	2

DECEMBER

S	M	T	W	TH	F	S
26	27	28	29	30	1	2
3	4	5	6	7	8	9
10	11	12	13	14	15	16
17	18	19	20	21	22	23
24	25	26	27	28	29	30
31						

2024

JANUARY

S	M	T	W	TH	F	S
31	1	2	3	4	5	6
7	8	9	10	11	12	13
14	15	16	17	18	19	20
21	22	23	24	25	26	27
28	29	30	31	1	2	3

FEBRUARY

S	M	T	W	TH	F	S
28	29	30	31	1	2	3
4	5	6	7	8	9	10
11	12	13	14	15	16	17
18	19	20	21	22	23	24
25	26	27	28	1	2	3

MARCH

S	M	T	W	TH	F	S
24	25	26	27	28	1	2
3	4	5	6	7	8	9
10	11	12	13	14	15	16
17	18	19	20	21	22	23
24	25	26	27	28	29	30
31						

APRIL

S	M	T	W	TH	F	S
31	1	2	3	4	5	6
7	8	9	10	11	12	13
14	15	16	17	18	19	20
21	22	23	24	25	26	27
28	29	30				

MAY

S	M	T	W	TH	F	S
28	29	30	1	2	3	4
5	6	7	8	9	10	11
12	13	14	15	16	17	18
19	20	21	22	23	24	25
26	27	28	29	30	31	

JUNE

S	M	T	W	TH	F	S
26	27	28	29	30	31	1
2	3	4	5	6	7	8
9	10	11	12	13	14	15
16	17	18	19	20	21	22
23	24	25	26	27	28	29
30						

JULY

S	M	T	W	TH	F	S
30	1	2	3	4	5	6
7	8	9	10	11	12	13
14	15	16	17	18	19	20
21	22	23	24	25	26	27
28	29	30	31			

AUGUST

S	M	T	W	TH	F	S
28	29	30	31	1	2	3
4	5	6	7	8	9	10
11	12	13	14	15	16	17
18	19	20	21	22	23	24
25	26	27	28	29	30	31

SEPTEMBER

S	M	T	W	TH	F	S
1	2	3	4	5	6	7
8	9	10	11	12	13	14
15	16	17	18	19	20	21
22	23	24	25	26	27	28
29	30					

OCTOBER

S	M	T	W	TH	F	S
28	30	1	2	3	4	5
6	7	8	9	10	11	12
13	14	15	16	17	18	19
20	21	22	23	24	25	26
27	28	29	30	31		

NOVEMBER

S	M	T	W	TH	F	S
27	28	29	30	31	1	2
3	4	5	6	7	8	9
10	11	12	13	14	15	16
17	18	19	20	21	22	23
24	25	26	27	28	29	30

DECEMBER

S	M	T	W	TH	F	S
1	2	3	4	5	6	7
8	9	10	11	12	13	14
15	16	17	18	19	20	21
22	23	24	25	26	27	28
29	30	31				

SUNDAY JANUARY 1

_____

_____

_____

_____

_____

_____

_____

MONDAY JANUARY 2

_____

_____

_____

_____

_____

_____

TUESDAY JANUARY 3

_____

_____

_____

_____

_____

_____

JANUARY 1, 1994 Zapatista forces overtake towns in Chiapas, beginning an ongoing revolution against the Mexican state. "The dispossessed, we are millions, and we thereby call upon our brothers and sisters to join this struggle as the only path."
—ZAPATISTA ARMY OF NATIONAL LIBERATION

JANUARY 1, 2009 Oscar Grant III was a twenty-two-year-old black man, fatally shot by an Oakland, California, transit cop in the early morning hours of the New Year. The riots that followed were some of the largest the United States had seen in decades. "Oscar Grant: Murdered. The Whole Damn System Is Guilty!"
—PLACARD FROM THE OSCAR GRANT REBELLION

JANUARY 5, 1971 Angela Davis—black feminist, philosopher, and prison abolitionist—declares her innocence in a California court over the kidnapping and murder of a judge. "Prisons do not disappear problems, they disappear human beings. And the practice of disappearing vast numbers of people from poor, immigrant, and racially marginalized communities has literally become big business."
—"MASKED RACISM"

JANUARY 7, 1957 Djamila Bouhired, the "Arab Joan of Arc" and member of the National Liberation Front, sets off a bomb in an Algiers café, precipitating the Battle of Algiers, a pivotal episode in the Algerian struggle for independence against the French. "It was the most beautiful day of my life because I was confident that I was going to be dying for the sake of the most wonderful story in the world."

WEDNESDAY JANUARY 4

_____

_____

_____

_____

_____

_____

_____

Subcomandante Marcos and Comandante Tacho in La Realidad, Chiapas, 1999

THURSDAY JANUARY 5

_____

_____

_____

_____

_____

_____

_____

NOTES:

_____

_____

_____

_____

_____

_____

FRIDAY JANUARY 6

_____

_____

_____

_____

_____

_____

_____

SATURDAY JANUARY 7

_____

_____

_____

_____

_____

_____

SUNDAY JANUARY 8

_____

_____

_____

_____

_____

_____

_____

_____

MONDAY JANUARY 9

_____

_____

_____

_____

_____

_____

_____

TUESDAY JANUARY 10

_____

_____

_____

_____

_____

_____

JANUARY 9, 1959 Rigoberta Menchú Tum, indigenous revolutionary and Nobel Peace Prize winner, is born in Chimel, Guatemala. "[My cause] wasn't born out of something good, it was born out of wretchedness and bitterness. It has been radicalized by the poverty in which my people live." —*I, RIGOBERTA MENCHÚ*

JANUARY 10, 1776 Thomas Paine, who participated in the American and French revolutions, publishes the pamphlet *Common Sense*, which argued for American independence from Britain. "Society in every state is a blessing, but government even in its best state is but a necessary evil; in its worst state an intolerable one."

JANUARY 11, 1894 Donghak Rebellion begins in Mujiang, Korea, over local corruption, eventually growing into an anti-establishment movement. "The people are the root of the nation. If the root withers, the nation will be enfeebled." —DONGHAK REBELLION PROCLAMATION

JANUARY 11, 1912 Workers in Lawrence, Massachusetts, walk out over a race-based pay cut in what would become known as the "bread and roses" strike. Soon an Industrial Workers of the World–organized strike shuts down every textile mill in the city.

JANUARY 13, 1898 Émile Zola publishes his infamous letter, "J'accuse...!," accusing the French government of framing Jewish general Alfred Dreyfus for sabotage.

JANUARY 12, 1904 Herero soldiers rebel against German colonial rule in present-day Namibia. It is estimated that the Herero population was reduced from 80,000 to 15,000 in the following three years through systematic violence and deportation.

WEDNESDAY JANUARY 11

_____

_____

_____

_____

_____

_____

_____

Rigoberta Menchú Tum, indigenous revolutionary and Nobel
Peace Prize winner

THURSDAY JANUARY 12

_____

_____

_____

_____

_____

_____

_____

NOTES:

_____

_____

_____

_____

_____

_____

FRIDAY JANUARY 13

_____

_____

_____

_____

_____

_____

_____

SATURDAY JANUARY 14

_____

_____

_____

_____

_____

_____

_____

SUNDAY JANUARY 15

———————————————————

———————————————————

———————————————————

———————————————————

———————————————————

———————————————————

———————————————————

———————————————————

MONDAY JANUARY 16

———————————————————

———————————————————

———————————————————

———————————————————

———————————————————

———————————————————

———————————————————

TUESDAY JANUARY 17

———————————————————

———————————————————

———————————————————

———————————————————

———————————————————

———————————————————

———————————————————

JANUARY 15, 1919 Rosa Luxemburg, founder of the Spartacus League, is murdered by the German Social Democratic government. "The madness will cease and the bloody demons of hell will vanish only when workers in Germany and France, England and Russia finally awake from their stupor, extend to each other a brotherly hand, and drown out the bestial chorus of imperialist war-mongers." —JUNIUS PAMPHLET

JANUARY 17, 1893 Queen Lili'uokalani, Hawaii's last monarch, is overthrown by American colonists.

JANUARY 17, 1961 Patrice Lumumba, Congolese independence leader and first prime minister of independent Congo, is assassinated by the Belgian government. Six months earlier, he had been deposed in a CIA-backed coup.

JANUARY 20, 1973 Amílcar Cabral, a communist intellectual and guerrilla leader of Guinea-Bissau's anti-colonial movement against the Portuguese, is assassinated. Guinea-Bissau became independent just months later. "Honesty, in a political context, is total commitment and total identification with the toiling masses."

JANUARY 20, 2017 Hundreds of protesters are arrested in Washington, DC as Donald Trump is inaugurated as US president, and the following day, an estimated 470,000 people rally for the Women's March on Washington.

JANUARY 21, 1935 The Wilderness Society is founded by conservationists; it would become one of the most radical US environmentalist groups into the 1970s. "Our bigger-and-better society is now like a hypochondriac, so obsessed with its own economic health as to have lost the capacity to remain healthy." —SOCIETY FOUNDER ALDO LEOPOLD, A SAND COUNTY ALMANAC

WEDNESDAY JANUARY 18

Patrice Lumumba (1925–1961) raises his unshackled arms
following his release, 1960

THURSDAY JANUARY 19

NOTES:

FRIDAY JANUARY 20

SATURDAY JANUARY 21

SUNDAY JANUARY 22

_____

_____

_____

_____

_____

_____

_____

MONDAY JANUARY 23

_____

_____

_____

_____

_____

_____

TUESDAY JANUARY 24

_____

_____

_____

_____

_____

_____

JANUARY 22, 1936 Burmese student union leaders Aung San and U Nu are expelled for criticizing British rule in Burma, leading to a national student strike. "Escaped from Awizi a devil in the form of a black dog ... Will finder please kick him back to hell." —NYO MYA, "A HELL HOUND AT LARGE"

JANUARY 23, 1976 Paul Robeson, the African-American singer and civil rights campaigner, dies. "I stand always on the side of those who will toil and labor. As an artist I come to sing, but as a citizen, I will always speak for peace, and no one can silence me in this."

JANUARY 24, 1911 The anarcho-feminist Kanno Sugako is hanged for plotting to assassinate Emperor Meiji. "In accordance with long-standing customs, we have been seen as a form of material property. Women in Japan are in a state of slavery." —"WOMEN ARE SLAVES"

JANUARY 27, 1924 Lenin's funeral takes place in Red Square. In attendance was the poet Vladimir Mayakovsky, who went on to pen the epic poem, "Vladimir Ilyich Lenin."

"Just guzzling
    snoozing
        and pocketing pelf,
Capitalism
    got lazy and feeble."

JANUARY 28, 1948 A plane crash kills twenty-eight bracero farm workers being sent back to Mexico. Cesar Chavez considered the moment part of his early political education.

"Who are all these friends, all scattered like dry leaves?
The radio says, 'They are just deportees ...'"
    —WOODY GUTHRIE, "DEPORTEE"

WEDNESDAY JANUARY 25

_____

_____

_____

_____

_____

_____

_____

Activist, singer, and actor Paul Robeson (1898–1976)

THURSDAY JANUARY 26

_____

_____

_____

_____

_____

_____

_____

NOTES:

_____

_____

_____

_____

_____

_____

FRIDAY JANUARY 27

_____

_____

_____

_____

_____

_____

_____

SATURDAY JANUARY 28

_____

_____

_____

_____

_____

_____

ABOLITION GEOGRAPHY
RUTH WILSON GILMORE

W. E. B. Du Bois interviewed Harriet Tubman late in her life. For a while in the mid twentieth century, a small but rather raucous scholarly competition developed to "prove" how many (which is to say how few) people Tubman helped "keep moving" along the Underground Railroad. By contrast, Harvard- and Humboldt-trained historian and sociologist Du Bois, a numbers guy if ever there was one, said hundreds. Then thousands! Why? Did he just get sloppy? Or did he begin to see how abolition geographies are made, on the ground, everywhere along the route—the time-route as well as the space-route. Indeed, was he able to redo in *Black Reconstruction in America* his earlier research on the Freedmen's Bureau because of the insights—truly visionary—he gained from talking with the ancient Tubman? It's here that I think the concept "infrastructure of feeling" might help us think about how we think about the development and perpetuation of abolition geographies, and how such geographies tend toward, even if they don't wholly achieve, the negation of the negation of the overlapping and

interlocking carceral geographies of which the prison-industrial complex is an exemplar—while absolutely nonexhaustive, as the examples of abolition geographies show.

Raymond Williams argued more than fifty years ago that each age has its own "structure of feeling," a narrative structure for understanding the dynamic material limits to the possibility of change. Paul Gilroy and many others have engaged Williams's thinking and shown that ages and places necessarily have multiple structures of feeling, which are dialectical rather than merely contemporaneous. Williams went on to explain how we might best understand tradition as an accumulation of structures of feeling—that gather not by chance, nor through a natural process that would seem like a drift or tide, but rather by way of what he calls the "selection and re-selection of ancestors." In this, Williams disavows the fixity of either culture or biology, discovering in perpetuation how even the least coherent aspects of human consciousness—feelings—have dynamically substantive shape.

The Black Radical Tradition is a constantly evolving accumulation of structures of feeling whose individual and collective narrative arcs persistently tend toward freedom. It is a way of mindful action that is constantly renewed and refreshed over time but maintains strength, speed, stamina, agility, flexibility, balance. The great explosions and distortions of modernity put into motion—and constant interaction—already existing as well as novel understandings of difference, possession, dependence, abundance. As a result, the selection and reselection of ancestors is itself part of the radical process of finding anywhere—if not everywhere—in political practice and analytical habit, lived expressions (including opacities) of unbounded participatory openness.

What underlies such accumulation? What is the productive capacity of visionary or crisis-driven or even exhaustion-provoked reselection? The best I can offer, until something better comes along, is what I've called for many years the "infrastructure of feeling." In the material world, infrastructure underlies productivity—it speeds some processes and slows down others, setting agendas, producing isolation, enabling cooperation. The infrastructure of feeling is material too, in the sense that ideology becomes material as do the actions that feelings enable or constrain. The infrastructure of feeling is then consciousness-foundation, sturdy but not static, that underlies our capacity to select, to recognize viscerally (no less than prudently) immanent possibility as we select and reselect liberatory lineages—in a lifetime, as Du Bois and Tubman exemplify, as well as between and across generations. What matters—what materializes—are lively re-articulations and surprising syncretisms. If, then, the structures of feeling for the Black Radical Tradition are, age upon age, shaped by energetically expectant consciousness of and direction toward unboundedness, then the tradition is, inexactly, movement away from partition and exclusion—indeed, its inverse.

This is a revised extract from Abolition Geography *by Ruth Wilson Gilmore (Verso, 2022).*

SUNDAY JANUARY 29

_____

_____

_____

_____

_____

_____

_____

_____

MONDAY JANUARY 30

_____

_____

_____

_____

_____

_____

_____

TUESDAY JANUARY 31

_____

_____

_____

_____

_____

_____

_____

JANUARY 29, 1967 Arusha Declaration, written by Julius Nyerere, is issued to clarify Tanzania's path toward Ujamaa, or African socialism. "We, in Africa, have no more need of being 'converted' to socialism than we have of being 'taught' democracy." —"UJAMAA, THE BASIS OF AFRICAN SOCIALISM"

JANUARY 30, 1972 British soldiers shot twenty-eight unarmed civilians in Northern Ireland during a peaceful protest march against internment, in what become known as Bloody Sunday—one of the most significant brutal events of The Troubles.

FEBRUARY 1, 1902 Langston Hughes, poet and figure of the Harlem Renaissance, is born.

"What happens to a dream deferred?
Does it dry up
like a raisin in the sun?
Or fester like a sore—
and then run?"
—"MONTAGE OF A DREAM DEFERRED"

FEBRUARY 2, 1512 Taíno hero Hatuey is captured and killed after besieging the Spaniards for four months at their first fort in Cuba. "[Gold] is the God the Spaniards worship. For these they fight and kill, for these they persecute us and that is why we have to throw them into the sea." —HATUEY'S SPEECH TO THE TAÍNOS

FEBRUARY 3, 1930 The Indochinese Communist Party is established; it conducted an underground struggle against the French colonialists and, later, the American invaders.

FEBRUARY 4, 1899 Philippine-American war begins after the Philippine government objects to being handed over to the US from Spain.

WEDNESDAY FEBRUARY 1

The 35th Bloody Sunday memorial march in Derry, 28 January 2007

THURSDAY FEBRUARY 2

NOTES:

FRIDAY FEBRUARY 3

SATURDAY FEBRUARY 4

SUNDAY FEBRUARY 5

MONDAY FEBRUARY 6

TUESDAY FEBRUARY 7

FEBRUARY 7, 1948 Tens of thousands of silent marchers in Bogotá memorialize victims of Colombian state violence. "Señor Presidente, our flag is in mourning; this silent multitude, the mute cry from our hearts, asks only that you treat us ... as you would have us treat you." —JORGE ELIÉCER GAITÁN, LEADER OF THE COLOMBIAN LIBERAL PARTY

FEBRUARY 8, 1677 Andrew Marvell, English poet and parliamentarian during the Anglo-Dutch wars, publishes his last known work. "There has now for divers years a design been carried on to change the lawful government of England into an absolute tyranny." —AN ACCOUNT OF THE GROWTH OF POPERY AND ARBITRARY GOVERNMENT IN ENGLAND

FEBRUARY 8, 1996 John Perry Barlow publishes "A Declaration of the Independence of Cyberspace" in response to an anti-pornography bill passed by the US Congress that would have chilled online speech dramatically. "On behalf of the future, I ask you of the past to leave us alone."

FEBRUARY 10, 1883 The Russian revolutionary Vera Figner is arrested for her role in Tsar Alexander II's assassination. She received a death sentence that was later commuted. "My past experience had convinced me that the only way to change the existing order was by force." —MEMOIRS OF A REVOLUTIONIST

FEBRUARY 11, 1916 Emma Goldman, anarchist agitator, publisher and all-around "rebel woman," is arrested for distributing a pamphlet about birth control written by Margaret Sanger.

FEBRUARY 11, 1990 Nelson Mandela is freed after twenty-seven years as a political prisoner. Four years later he became the first president of post-apartheid South Africa.

WEDNESDAY FEBRUARY 8

Vera Nikolayevna Figner (1852–1942) after the 1905 Russian Revolution

THURSDAY FEBRUARY 9

NOTES:

FRIDAY FEBRUARY 10

SATURDAY FEBRUARY 11

SUNDAY FEBRUARY 12

_____

_____

_____

_____

_____

_____

MONDAY FEBRUARY 13

_____

_____

_____

_____

_____

_____

_____

TUESDAY FEBRUARY 14

_____

_____

_____

_____

_____

_____

_____

FEBRUARY 13, 1967 Forough Farrokhzad, feminist poet who has inspired much debate in Iran about modernity, dies in a car crash. "If you want these bonds broken, grasp the skirt of obstinacy." —"CALL TO ARMS"

FEBRUARY 14, 1818 The birth date chosen by Frederick Douglass, America's foremost abolitionist writer and activist. "What, to the American slave, is your 4th of July? I answer: a day that reveals to him, more than all other days in the year, the gross injustice and cruelty to which he is the constant victim." —"THE MEANING OF JULY FOURTH FOR THE NEGRO"

FEBRUARY 15, 1855 Muktabai, a fourteen-year-old Dalit, publishes the earliest surviving piece of writing by an "untouchable" woman. "Let that religion, where only one person is privileged and the rest are deprived, perish from the earth and let it never enter our minds to be proud of such a religion." —"ABOUT THE GRIEFS OF THE MANGS AND MAHARS"

FEBRUARY 17, 1958 The Campaign for Nuclear Disarmament is founded in Britain; it would become the country's most important protest movement during the late 1950s and early 1960s. "Sanity is always hardest to restore at the summit—the air here is rarified. It seems to affect the brain. We can assert it at the base." —ACTIVIST ALEX COMFORT'S SPEECH AT THE INAUGURAL MEETING

FEBRUARY 18, 1934 Black lesbian poet Audre Lorde is born in New York City.

"For all of us
 this instant and this triumph
 We were never meant to survive."
    —"A LITANY FOR SURVIVAL"

WEDNESDAY FEBRUARY 15

Audre Lorde © Robert Alexander, 1983

THURSDAY FEBRUARY 16

NOTES:

FRIDAY FEBRUARY 17

SATURDAY FEBRUARY 18

SUNDAY FEBRUARY 19

_____

_____

_____

_____

_____

_____

_____

MONDAY FEBRUARY 20

_____

_____

_____

_____

_____

_____

TUESDAY FEBRUARY 21

_____

_____

_____

_____

_____

_____

FEBRUARY 19, 1942 Japanese American internment begins in the US through Executive Order 9066.

FEBRUARY 19, 1963 Betty Friedan's _The Feminine Mystique_, a classic of second-wave feminism, is published. "The problem lay buried, unspoken, for many years in the minds of American women."

FEBRUARY 21, 1848 The _Communist Manifesto_, written by Friedrich Engels and Karl Marx, is published. "The proletarians have nothing to lose but their chains. They have a world to win."

FEBRUARY 21, 1965 Malcolm X is assassinated at the Audubon Ballroom in New York City. "Uncle Sam's hands are dripping with blood, dripping with the blood of the black man in this country." —"THE BALLOT OR THE BULLET"

FEBRUARY 23, 1848 French revolutionaries overthrow the Orléans monarchy and establish the Second Republic, where socialist Louis Blanc attempts to implement worker cooperatives. "What does competition mean to working men? It is the distribution of work to the highest bidder." —"THE ORGANIZATION OF LABOUR"

FEBRUARY 23, 1934 George Padmore, leading Pan-Africanist born in Trinidad, is expelled from the Comintern and shifts his focus to African independence struggles. "The black man certainly has to pay dear for carrying the white man's burden." —"THE WHITE MAN'S BURDEN"

FEBRUARY 24, 1895 Cuba's final War of Independence from Spain begins, planned in part by poet and revolutionary philosopher José Martí. "A cloud of ideas is a thing no armored prow can smash through." —"OUR AMERICA"

WEDNESDAY FEBRUARY 22

Malcolm X (1925–1965) by Ed Ford, World Telegram staff
photographer

THURSDAY FEBRUARY 23

NOTES:

FRIDAY FEBRUARY 24

SATURDAY FEBRUARY 25

THE EYEBALL BUSINESS
BEN TARNOFF

In 1998, the same year that eBay burst onto the Nasdaq, a pair of graduate students presented a paper at an academic conference. The paper described a search engine they had built at Stanford. It was still a prototype—it ran on a set of scavenged and thrifted computers in a dorm room—but a prototype that had become so popular that, at peak times, it used half of the university's internet bandwidth. The students called it Google. That year, they founded a company of the same name.

The story of Google has been told many times before. It has been celebrated and emulated, critiqued and parodied. But what has receded in the telling and retelling of this story is the original problem that the young Larry Page and Sergey Brin were trying to solve. This is the problem of having too much data.

Having too much data was one of many scenarios unforeseen by the internet's architects. The idea that someday there would be billions of people and tens of billions of devices all bound together through the protocol they were creating was well beyond imagining. Their best guess at the outer bound of how many IP addresses they would ever need—the unique identifiers assigned to computers connected to the internet—was about 4.3 billion. Even that seemed excessive to some: the programmer Virginia Strazisar Travers, who played a central role in the internet's creation, later remembered thinking that 65,536 would be enough for her lifetime.

In the 1990s, the situation looked different. Tens of millions of people were joining the internet each year. Millions of miles of fiber-optic cable were being laid. And prodigious amounts of data were being manufactured, particularly on the World Wide Web, where newcomers congregated. The number of websites grew nearly 1,000 percent from 1995 to 1996.

In theory, more information should have made the web more useful. In practice, more information made the web more bewildering. The existing tools for making sense of it all simply weren't up to the job. Yahoo!'s reliance on humans—the fact that its listings were manually curated—meant that it struggled to keep pace with the growth of the web. Automated alternatives existed—"web crawlers" that indexed sites to make them searchable—but they weren't very good, often returning useless and spammy results.

This was the challenge that Page and Brin aimed to overcome, with funding from DARPA and the National Science Foundation—the agency that had created the internet and the agency that had run it until recently. "The number of documents in the [search engine] indices has been increasing by many orders of magnitude," they wrote in their 1998 paper, "but the user's ability to look at documents has not." Their solution was an algorithmic method for ranking the quality and relevance of a webpage that relied primarily on counting how many other sites linked to it. This tended to produce more pertinent results and, crucially, it scaled well. A vast and rapidly expanding patchwork would be made more intelligible through an automated analysis of how it was all sewn together.

But as Google moved off-campus and became a business and grew, something else happened. It began not only to organize the data of the web but to generate a fair bit of its own. Everything that users did left footprints in the servers' logs: what they searched for, when they searched for it, what results they clicked on, whether they stayed there or returned to start a new search. And the footprints added up: by November 1999, Google was processing more than 4 million searches a day.

The company began using this data to improve its search engine. By studying user behavior, engineers could identify gaps and glitches in the software, and remake the ranking algorithm to respond to a range of new signals. Then, in the early 2000s, the company started using the data for another purpose: to sell ads.

This is a revised extract from Internet for the People: The Fight for Our Digital Future *by Ben Tarnoff (Verso, 2022).*

SUNDAY FEBRUARY 26

_____

_____

_____

_____

_____

_____

_____

MONDAY FEBRUARY 27

_____

_____

_____

_____

_____

_____

TUESDAY FEBRUARY 28

_____

_____

_____

_____

_____

_____

FEBRUARY 26, 1906 Upton Sinclair's exposé on the meat packing industry, _The Jungle_, is published, prompting the enactment of the Meat Inspection and Pure Food and Drug Acts.

FEBRUARY 27, 1832 Auguste Blanqui, French revolutionary and early theorist of class struggle, is found guilty (with fourteen others) of supporting republicanism. "This is the war between the rich and the poor: the rich wanted it so, for they are the aggressors. But they find it wrong that the poor fight back." —BLANQUI'S DEFENSE SPEECH

FEBRUARY 27, 1973 Oglala Lakota and American Indian Movement members, including Leonard Peltier, begin an occupation of Wounded Knee, South Dakota on the Pine Ridge Indian Reservation.

MARCH 1, 1896 Ethiopian fighters defeat Italian forces at the Battle of Adwa, securing Ethiopian sovereignty to become a symbol of African resistance against European colonialism. "Once a white snake has bitten you, you will find no cure for it." —ETHIOPIAN REBEL LEADER BAHTA HAGOS

MARCH 1, 1940 Richard Wright's seminal novel _Native Son_, about a black youth living on Chicago's South Side, is published. His writings would shift the US discourse on race.

MARCH 1, 1954 Lolita Lebrón and comrades open fire on the US House of Representatives in the struggle for Puerto Rican independence. "I did not come to kill anyone, I came to die for Puerto Rico." —LEBRÓN, WORDS UPON ARREST

MARCH 2, 1444 Albanian resistance leader Skanderbeg founds the League of Lezhë, uniting Balkan chieftains to fight the invading Ottoman army.

WEDNESDAY MARCH 1

Lolita Lebrón (1919–2010) following her arrest in 1954

THURSDAY MARCH 2

NOTES:

FRIDAY MARCH 3

SATURDAY MARCH 4

SUNDAY MARCH 5

_____

_____

_____

_____

_____

_____

_____

MONDAY MARCH 6

_____

_____

_____

_____

_____

_____

_____

TUESDAY MARCH 7

_____

_____

_____

_____

_____

_____

_____

MARCH 6, 1923 The Egyptian Feminist Union is established. "They rise in times of trouble when the wills of men are tried." —ACTIVIST HUDA SHAARAWI, *HAREM YEARS: THE MEMOIRS OF AN EGYPTIAN FEMINIST, 1879–1924*

MARCH 6, 1957 The leader of the Gold Coast's imperialism fight against the British, Pan-Africanist Kwame Nkrumah, becomes the first prime minister of independent Ghana.

MARCH 6, 1984 Coal miners walk out at Cortonwood Colliery in South Yorkshire, beginning the yearlong UK miner's strike, the longest in history. "I'd rather be a picket than a scab." —PICKET LINE SLOGAN

MARCH 7, 1921 At the Kronstadt naval base, Russia's Red Army attacks sailors, soldiers and civilians who are protesting widespread famine and the Bolshevik repression of strikes. "This unrest shows clearly enough that the party has lost the faith of the working masses." —PETROPAVLOVSK RESOLUTION AND DEMANDS

MARCH 7, 1942 Lucy Parsons, anarchist and Industrial Workers of the World cofounder who was born in slavery, dies in Chicago. "Stroll you down the avenues of the rich and look through the magnificent plate windows into their voluptuous homes, and here you will discover the *very identical robbers* who have despoiled you and yours." —"TO TRAMPS"

MARCH 8, 1914 First International Women's Day, cofounded by German Marxist Clara Zetkin, is established on this day of the year. "What made women's labour particularly attractive to the capitalists was not only its lower price but also the greater submissiveness of women."

WEDNESDAY MARCH 8

Lucy Parsons (1853–1942) after her arrest for rioting at a 1915 unemployment protest

THURSDAY MARCH 9

NOTES:

FRIDAY MARCH 10

SATURDAY MARCH 11

SUNDAY MARCH 12

_____

_____

_____

_____

_____

_____

MONDAY MARCH 13

_____

_____

_____

_____

_____

_____

TUESDAY MARCH 14

_____

_____

_____

_____

_____

_____

MARCH 13, 1933 The poet Abdukhaliq Uyghur is executed by the Chinese government for encouraging rebellion and supporting Uyghur independence.

MARCH 13, 1979 Maurice Bishop's New Jewel Movement overthrows the Grenada government, the first armed socialist revolution in a predominantly black country outside of Africa.

MARCH 14, 2008 Riots break out in Lhasa and spread throughout Tibet, targeting Han Chinese residents and businesses. "The oppressors' snipers are still standing above Tibetan people's heads; on sunny days, the beams deflected from the guns in their hands stab into the prostrating Tibetans. This is a collective memory which has been engraved on Tibetan people's hearts."
—TIBETAN POET WOESER

MARCH 15, 1845 Friedrich Engels publishes _The Condition of the Working Class in England._

MARCH 15, 1960 A student demonstration against the fraudulent election victory of South Korean strongman Syngman Rhee was attacked by police. One month later, the body of student protester Kim Ju-yul washed ashore, his skull split open by a tear-gas grenade. The public outrage would eventually result in the April Revolution, which would end Rhee's rule.

MARCH 18, 1834 Six farm workers from Tolpuddle, England, are sentenced to penal transportation to Australia for forming a trade union.

MARCH 18, 1871 Paris Commune is established, a participatory workers' democracy. "Workers, make no mistake—this is an all-out war, a war between parasites and workers, exploiters and producers."
—COMMUNARDS, "DECLARATION BY THE CENTRAL COMMITTEE OF THE NATIONAL GUARD"

WEDNESDAY MARCH 15

Paris Commune: a barricade on Rue Voltaire, after its capture by the regular army during the Bloody Week

THURSDAY MARCH 16

NOTES:

FRIDAY MARCH 17

SATURDAY MARCH 18

SUNDAY MARCH 19

_____

_____

_____

_____

_____

_____

_____

MONDAY MARCH 20

_____

_____

_____

_____

_____

_____

_____

TUESDAY MARCH 21

_____

_____

_____

_____

_____

_____

_____

MARCH 21, 1960 South African police kill sixty-nine protesters in the Sharpeville Massacre, forcing the anti-apartheid movement underground.

MARCH 23, 1918 Avant-garde artist Tristan Tzara issues the Dada Manifesto, a politico-artistic movement whose anti-bourgeois stance would influence the Situationists and the Beats. "DADA DADA DADA—the roar of contorted pains, the interweaving of contraries and all contradictions, freaks and irrelevancies: LIFE."

MARCH 23, 1931 Revolutionary Bhagat Singh, who threw a bomb into India's central legislative assembly, is hanged by the British Raj. "Let me tell you, British rule is here not because God wills it but because they possess power and we do not dare to oppose them." —"WHY AM I AN ATHEIST?"

MARCH 24, 1977 Argentine journalist Rodolfo Walsh publishes his "Open Letter from a Writer to the Military Junta," accusing them of disappearing thousands of Argentines. The next day he is murdered. "They are the victims of a doctrine of collective guilt, which long ago disappeared from the norms of justice of any civilized community."

MARCH 24, 1980 Oscar Romero, archbishop of San Salvador in El Salvador and critic of the Salvadorean death squads, is assassinated while giving mass. "We are your people. The peasants you kill are your own brothers and sisters."

MARCH 24, 1987 First demonstration of ACT UP, pioneering direct-action AIDS organization, on Wall Street to protest Food and Drug Administration inaction on drug development. "Silence = Death" —ACT UP LOGO

WEDNESDAY MARCH 22

SILENCE=DEATH

The iconic poster of ACT UP, 1987

THURSDAY MARCH 23

NOTES:

FRIDAY MARCH 24

SATURDAY MARCH 25

SUNDAY MARCH 26

MARCH 27, 1969 First national Chicano Youth Conference is hosted in Denver by Crusade for Justice, the civil rights organization founded by former boxer Corky Gonzáles.

> "I have come a long way to nowhere,
> unwillingly dragged by that
> monstrous, technical,
> industrial giant
> called
> Progress
> and Anglo success ..."
> —GONZÁLES, "I AM JOAQUIN"

MONDAY MARCH 27

MARCH 29, 1942 The Hukbalahap (Philippine communist guerrilla organization) is founded; its insurgency against the government lasts eight years. "Our friends in Manila refer to us as being 'outside.' That is incorrect terminology... We are on the inside of the struggle." —PEASANT LEADER LUIS TARUC, *BORN OF THE PEOPLE*

MARCH 30, 1892 Freethinker Robert Ingersoll, favorite orator of Walt Whitman, delivers a eulogy for the poet after his death. "Whoever produces anything by weary labor, does not need a revelation from heaven to teach him that he has a right to the thing produced." —INGERSOLL, "SOME MISTAKES OF MOSES"

TUESDAY MARCH 28

APRIL 1, 1649 Poor farmers begin digging plots at Saint George's Hill in Surrey, in one of the first acts of the Digger movement that sought to abolish property and wages, in some instances by occupying common land. "We are resolved to be cheated no longer, nor be held under the slavish fear of you no longer, seeing the Earth was made for us, as well as for you." —MOVEMENT FOUNDER GERRARD WINSTANLEY, "DECLARATION FROM THE POOR OPPRESSED PEOPLE OF ENGLAND"

WEDNESDAY MARCH 29

Rodolfo "Corky" Gonzáles, Mexican American boxer, poet, and political activist.

THURSDAY MARCH 30

NOTES:

FRIDAY MARCH 31

SATURDAY APRIL 1

Taking Back Resources by Sanya Hyland
(Dissenters/wearedissenters.org)

Cancel Rent by Stephanie Monohan
(stephaniemonohan.com)

SUNDAY APRIL 2

_____

_____

_____

_____

_____

_____

_____

MONDAY APRIL 3

_____

_____

_____

_____

_____

_____

_____

TUESDAY APRIL 4

_____

_____

_____

_____

_____

_____

_____

APRIL 3, 1874 Wong Chin Foo, publisher of the first Chinese American newspaper, is naturalized as a US citizen. "The difference between the heathen and the Christian is that the heathen does good for the sake of doing good."

APRIL 3, 1895 Playwright and essayist Oscar Wilde goes on trial for homosexual activity and is imprisoned for two years. "It is immoral to use private property in order to alleviate the horrible evils that result from the institution of private property." —"THE SOUL OF MAN UNDER SOCIALISM"

APRIL 4, 1968 Martin Luther King, Jr. is assassinated. "A true revolution of values will soon look uneasily on the glaring contrast of poverty and wealth." —"BEYOND VIETNAM: A TIME TO BREAK SILENCE"

APRIL 5, 1971 The "Manifesto of the 343," signed by 343 women (including Simone de Beauvoir) who had had secret abortions, demands that the French government legalize the procedure.

APRIL 5, 1976 On the traditional day of mourning, thousands of Beijingers lay wreaths and poems on Tiananmen Square, indirectly criticizing the Cultural Revolution.

"If a thousand challengers lie beneath your feet,
Count me as number thousand and one."
—BEI DAO, "THE ANSWER," WHICH BECAME AN ANTHEM OF THE DEMOCRACY MOVEMENT

APRIL 8, 1950 Imprisoned for sedition, the revolutionary Turkish poet Nazim Hikmet launches a hunger strike for amnesty for political prisoners.

"Galloping from farthest Asia
and jutting into the Mediterranean
like a mare's head
this country is ours."
—"INVITATION"

WEDNESDAY APRIL 5

_____
_____
_____
_____
_____
_____
_____

Dr. Martin Luther King, Jr. (1929–1968) being arrested in 1956 during the Montgomery Bus Boycott

THURSDAY APRIL 6

_____
_____
_____
_____
_____
_____
_____

NOTES:

_____
_____
_____
_____
_____
_____

FRIDAY APRIL 7

_____
_____
_____
_____
_____
_____

SATURDAY APRIL 8

_____
_____
_____
_____
_____
_____

SUNDAY APRIL 9

APRIL 10, 1919 Emiliano Zapata, Mexican Revolution leader, is assassinated by the government. "The nation is tired of false men and traitors who make promises like liberators and who on arriving in power forget them and constitute themselves as tyrants."

APRIL 11, 1981 Riots break out in the Caribbean London neighborhood of Brixton in response to police targeting of young black men under the Sus law. The fighting lasts for three days.

APRIL 11, 2007 Kurt Vonnegut, author of novels with anti-authoritarian and anti-war themes, dies.

MONDAY APRIL 10

APRIL 13, 1635 Fakhr al-Din II, Druze independence leader against the Ottoman Empire and Lebanon's first freedom fighter, is executed. "No promise of reward or threat of punishment will dissuade us." —MESSAGE TO THE PEOPLE

APRIL 14, 1428 Vietnamese forces are victorious after a ten-year rebellion against their Chinese rulers. "Today it is a case of the grasshopper pitted against the elephant. But tomorrow the elephant will have its guts ripped out." —REBELLION LEADER LÊ LỢI'S VICTORY SPEECH

APRIL 14, 2002 Venezuelan president Hugo Chávez, who described his socialist movement as the Bolivarian Revolution, returns to power after having been ousted in a US-backed coup two days earlier. "What we now have to do is define the future of the world. Dawn is breaking out all over." —ADDRESS TO THE UN GENERAL ASSEMBLY

TUESDAY APRIL 11

APRIL 15, 1936 The Great Revolt begins in Palestine against British Mandate and Zionism, lasting three years. "They stepped all over us until we couldn't take any more. This went on until the rebellion was smashed." —MAHMOUD ABOU DEEB, WITNESS TO THE REVOLT

WEDNESDAY APRIL 12

The Brixton Riots, 1981

THURSDAY APRIL 13

NOTES:

FRIDAY APRIL 14

SATURDAY APRIL 15

SUNDAY APRIL 16

MONDAY APRIL 17

TUESDAY APRIL 18

APRIL 18, 1955 Twenty-nine newly independent African and Asian countries meet at the Bandung Conference in Indonesia, in a show of strength for the Non-Aligned Movement. "Without peace, our independence means little." —OPENING SPEECH BY INDONESIAN LEADER SUKARNO

APRIL 20, 1773 Peter Bestes and others deliver a petition for freedom "in behalf of our fellow slaves" to the Massachusetts legislature. "The divine spirit of freedom seems to fire every human breast on the continent, except such as are bribed to assist in executing the execrable plan."

APRIL 21, 1913 The Indian revolutionary group, the Ghadar Party, is formed by Punjabis in North America. "The nation-state may truly be compared to the dinosaurs and the tyrannosaurus of the Mesozoic Age. Like those gigantic reptiles, the modern nation-state has a very small brain with which to think and plan, but tremendously powerful teeth with which to tear and rend, to destroy and dismember." —FOUNDER LALA HAR DAYAL, "HINTS OF SELF-CULTURE"

APRIL 21, 1913 The Indian revolutionary group, the Ghadar Party, is formed by Punjabis in North America. "The nation-state may truly be compared to the dinosaurs and the tyrannosaurus of the Mesozoic Age. Like those gigantic reptiles, the modern nation-state has a very small brain with which to think and plan, but tremendously powerful teeth with which to tear and rend, to destroy and dismember." —FOUNDER LALA HAR DAYAL, "HINTS OF SELF-CULTURE"

APRIL 22, 1977 Kenyan activist Wangari Maathai founds the Green Belt Movement, an environmental nonprofit aimed at empowering poor, rural women. "Until you dig a hole, you plant a tree, you water it and make it survive, you haven't done a thing."

WEDNESDAY APRIL 19

UC Berkeley students of the Ghadar Movement, 1915

THURSDAY APRIL 20

NOTES:

FRIDAY APRIL 21

SATURDAY APRIL 22

_____

_____

_____

_____

_____

_____

_____

_____

_____

_____

_____

_____

_____

_____

_____

_____

_____

_____

_____

_____

_____

APRIL 23, 1968 Students occupy buildings in New York's Columbia University to protest the school's ties to a defense contractor, triggering a campus-wide strike. "Up against the wall, Motherfuckers!" —PROTEST GRAFFITI

APRIL 24, 1916 Irish republicans mount an armed insurrection against the British imperialists on Easter week, in what became known as the Easter Rising.

APRIL 25, 1974 Portuguese armed forces overthrow the ruling Estado Novo dictatorship in what becomes known as the Carnation Revolution, setting the stage for its colonies to achieve independence.

APRIL 26, 1937 The Basque town of Guernica is destroyed in an aerial bombing by German and Italian forces, in one of the most sordid episodes of the Spanish Civil War.

"Faces good in firelight good in frost
Refusing the night the wounds and blows."
—SURREALIST POET PAUL ELUARD, "VICTORY OF GUERNICA"

APRIL 28, 1967 Heavyweight champion boxer Muhammad Ali refuses induction into the US Armed Forces, leading to a charge for draft evasion and being stripped of his titles. "I ain't got no quarrel with them Vietcong. No Vietcong ever called me nigger."

APRIL 29, 1992 Los Angeles residents begin rioting after the four police officers accused of beating Rodney King are acquitted. "Give us the hammer and the nails, we will rebuild the city." —BLOODS AND CRIPS, "PLAN FOR THE RECONSTRUCTION OF LOS ANGELES"

WEDNESDAY APRIL 26

POBLACHT NA H EIREANN.
THE PROVISIONAL GOVERNMENT
OF THE
IRISH REPUBLIC
TO THE PEOPLE OF IRELAND.

IRISHMEN AND IRISHWOMEN : In the name of God and of the dead generations from which she receives her old tradition of nationhood, Ireland, through us, summons her children to her flag and strikes for her freedom.

Having organised and trained her manhood through her secret revolutionary organisation, the Irish Republican Brotherhood, and through her open military organisations, the Irish Volunteers and the Irish Citizen Army, having patiently perfected her discipline, having resolutely waited for the right moment to reveal itself, she now seizes that moment, and, supported by her exiled children in America and by gallant allies in Europe, but relying in the first on her own strength, she strikes in full confidence of victory.

We declare the right of the people of Ireland to the ownership of Ireland, and to the unfettered control of Irish destinies, to be sovereign and indefeasible. The long usurpation of that right by a foreign people and government has not extinguished the right, nor can it ever be extinguished except by the destruction of the Irish people. In every generation the Irish people have asserted their right to national freedom and sovereignty; six times during the past three hundred years they have asserted it in arms. Standing on that fundamental right and again asserting it in arms in the face of the world, we hereby proclaim the Irish Republic as a Sovereign Independent State, and we pledge our lives and the lives of our comrades-in-arms to the cause of its freedom, of its welfare, and of its exaltation among the nations.

The Proclamation of the Irish Republic, 1916

THURSDAY APRIL 27

NOTES:

FRIDAY APRIL 28

SATURDAY APRIL 29

ABOLISH THE FAMILY
SOPHIE LEWIS

Most family abolitionists love their families. It is true of course that it is usually the people who have had bad experiences within a social system, and who feel things *besides* love for that system, who initiate movements to overthrow it. But loving one's family in spite of a "hard childhood" is actually pretty typical of the would-be family abolitionist. She may, for instance, sense in her gut that she and the members of her family simply aren't *good* for each other, while also loving them, wishing them joy, and knowing full well that there are *few or no* available alternatives in this world when it comes to providing much-needed care for everybody in question. Frankly, loving one's family can be a problem *for anyone*. It might put extra weights around the ankles of a domestic battery survivor seeking to escape (especially given the economic punishments imposed by capitalism on those who flee commodified housing). It might hinder a trans or disabled child from claiming medical care. It might dissuade someone from getting an abortion. Right now, few would deny that reproductive *rights*—let alone justice—are everywhere

systematically denied to populations. Austerity policies purposively render proletarian baby-making crushingly unaffordable, even for two or three or four adults working together, let alone one. Housework is sexed, racialized and (except in the houses of the rich) unwaged. It is unsurprising, in these global conditions, that large numbers of humans do not or *cannot* love their families. Reasons range from simple incompatibility to various phobias, ableism, sexual violence, and neglect.

Let me tell you a secret: people get really angry when you suggest to them that they deserved better than what they got growing up. And I've noticed that a lot of people have the "*but I love my family*" reaction with the most startling vehemence immediately after they've spent a long time talking freely to me about the strain, tragedy, blackmail and care-starved frustration that characterized their "biological" upbringing. Angry opposition to the idea that *things could be different* comes, I've found, right after we have voiced the wish that relatives of ours could have been less alone, less burdened by caring responsibilities, less trapped. Those people are quite another matter, this defensive spasm seems to say: I, myself, don't need any family abolition, thank you very much. Sure, it may be a disciplinary, scarcity-based trauma-machine: but it's MY disciplinary, scarcity-based trauma-machine.

Listen. I get it. It's not just that you're worried about your dad getting all upset if he sees you with this book. It's that it's existentially petrifying to imagine relinquishing the organized poverty we have in favor of an abundance we have never known and have yet to organize.

What is the family? So deep runs the idea that the family is the exclusive place where people are safe, where people come from, where people are made, and where people belong, it doesn't even feel like an idea anymore. Let us unpick it, then.

The family is the reason we are supposed to want to go to work, the reason we have to go to work, and the reason we *can* go to work. As every civic-minded individual's raison d'être par excellence, "family" is an ostensibly non-individualist creed: an unselfish principle one voluntarily signs up to without thinking about it. What alternative could there be? The economic assumption that behind every "breadwinner" there is a private someone (or someones) worth being exploited for, notably some kind of wife—i.e., a person who is likely a breadwinner too, and possibly even *the same person*—"freely" making sandwiches with the hard-won bread, or hiring someone else to do so, vacuuming up the crumbs, and

refrigerating leftovers, such that more bread can be won tomorrow: this feels to many of us like a description of "human nature."

Without the family, who or what would take responsibility for the lives of non-workers, including the ill, the young, and the elderly? This question is a bad one. We don't hesitate to say that animals are better off outside of zoos, even if they have become used to the abuse of zoos. Similarly: transition out of the family will be tricky, yes, but the family is doing a bad job at care, and we all deserve better. The family is getting in the way of alternatives.

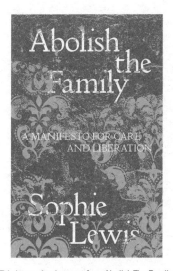

This is a revised extract from Abolish The Family: A Manifesto for Care and Liberation *by Sophie Lewis (Verso, 2022).*

SUNDAY APRIL 30

MONDAY MAY 1

TUESDAY MAY 2

MAY 1, 1949 Albert Einstein publishes "Why Socialism?" in the inaugural issue of *Monthly Review*. "The economic anarchy of capitalist society as it exists today is, in my opinion, the real source of the evil."

MAY 1, 1970 Lesbian activists deliver their manifesto at the Second Congress to Unite Women in New York City, to protest the exclusion of lesbian speakers. "Lesbian is a label invented by the man to throw at any woman who dares to be his equal." —RADICALESBIANS, "THE WOMAN-IDENTIFIED WOMAN"

MAY 4, 1886 At a rally for the eight-hour day at Haymarket Square in Chicago, a bomb is thrown at police and eight anarchists are later convicted of conspiracy. "I repeat that I am the enemy of the 'order' of today, and I repeat that, with all my powers, so long as breath remains in me, I shall combat it." —LOUIS LINGG'S TRIAL SPEECH

MAY 4, 1919 Chinese students demonstrate in Beijing, sparking the anti-Confucian New Culture Movement. "Wanting to eat men, at the same time afraid of being eaten themselves, they all eye each other with the deepest suspicion." —LU XUN, *A MADMAN'S DIARY*, ONE OF THE MOVEMENT'S REPRESENTATIVE WORKS

MAY 5, 1938 Second and final arrest of Russian poet Osip Mandelstam, for writing critically of Stalin.

"He forges decrees in a line like horseshoes
One for the groin, one the forehead, temple, eye"
—"THE STALIN EPIGRAM"

MAY 5, 1966 Jit Poumisak, Thai Marxist poet and revolutionary, is killed after retreating to the jungle with the outlawed Communist Party. "[The Thai people] have been able to identify clearly the enemies who plunder them and skin them alive and suck the very marrow from their bones." —"THE REAL FACE OF THAI SAKTINA [FEUDALISM] TODAY"

WEDNESDAY MAY 3

THURSDAY MAY 4

FRIDAY MAY 5

SATURDAY MAY 6

Attention Workingmen!

GREAT

MASS-MEETING

TO-NIGHT, at 7.30 o'clock,

AT THE

HAYMARKET, Randolph St., Bet. Desplaines and Halsted.

Good Speakers will be present to denounce the latest atrocious act of the police, the shooting of our fellow-workmen yesterday afternoon.

Workingmen Arm Yourselves and Appear in Full Force!

THE EXECUTIVE COMMITTEE.

Achtung, Arbeiter!

The first flier calling for a rally in the Haymarket on May 4, 1886

NOTES:

SUNDAY MAY 7

_____

_____

_____

_____

_____

_____

_____

MONDAY MAY 8

_____

_____

_____

_____

_____

_____

TUESDAY MAY 9

_____

_____

_____

_____

_____

_____

_____

MAY 9, 1918 Scottish revolutionary John Maclean, on trial for sedition for opposing WWI, delivers a rousing speech from the dock. "I am here as the accuser of capitalism, dripping with blood from head to foot."

MAY 11, 1930 Pedro Albizu Campos is elected president of the Puerto Rican Nationalist Party. "The empire is a system. It can wait. It can fatten its victims to render its digestion more enjoyable at a later time."

MAY 10, 1857 Rebellion against British rule in India begins, eventually growing into the First Indian War of Independence.

MAY 10, 1872 Victoria Woodhull, suffragist and publisher of the first English edition of _The Communist Manifesto_, becomes the first woman nominated for president of the US.

MAY 11, 1894 Three thousand employees of the Pullman railcar company go on strike, eventually growing to 250,000 workers before being crushed by federal troops.

MAY 12, 1916 James Connolly is tied to a chair and shot by the British government for his role in the Easter Rising—the precursor to the declaration of the Irish Republic in 1919. Born in Scotland to Irish immigrant parents, Connolly became a leader of the socialist movement in Scotland, Ireland and the United States, where he was a member of the Socialist Party and the IWW.

MAY 13, 1968 French workers join students in a one-day strike, with over a million protesters marching through Paris streets. By the following week, two-thirds of France's workforce was on strike, becoming the largest general strike that had ever stopped the economy of an industrialized country.

WEDNESDAY MAY 10

Victoria Woodhull, suffragist and publisher of the first English edition of *The Communist Manifesto*

THURSDAY MAY 11

NOTES:

FRIDAY MAY 12

SATURDAY MAY 13

SUNDAY MAY 14

_____

_____

_____

_____

_____

_____

_____

MONDAY MAY 15

_____

_____

_____

_____

_____

_____

_____

TUESDAY MAY 16

_____

_____

_____

_____

_____

_____

_____

MAY 16, 1943 Warsaw Ghetto Uprising, which began in German-occupied Poland to resist the last deportation of Jews to the Treblinka extermination camp, ends in failure. "We decided to gamble for our lives." —MAREK EDELMAN, MEMBER OF THE JEWISH COMBAT ORGANIZATION

MAY 17, 1649 A mutiny in the New Model Army of England by the Levellers, who called for the expansion of suffrage, religious toleration, and sweeping political reforms, is crushed when its leaders are executed. "We do now hold ourselves bound in mutual duty to each other to take the best care we can for the future to avoid both the danger of returning into a slavish condition and the chargeable remedy of another war." —LEVELLERS, "AGREEMENT OF THE PEOPLE"

MAY 18, 1980 Citizens of Kwangju, South Korea, seize control of their city, demanding democratization, an end to martial law, and an increase in the minimum wage.

MAY 19, 1869 US president Ulysses S. Grant issues the National Eight Hour Law Proclamation, an early but symbolic victory for the struggle over the working day in the US. "Think carefully of the difference between the operative and the mechanic leaving his work at half-past seven (after dark, the most of the year), and that of the more leisurely walk home at half-past four p.m., or three hours earlier." —MACHINIST-TURNED-ACTIVIST IRA STEWARD, "THE EIGHT HOUR MOVEMENT"

MAY 19, 1946 Millions of Japanese take part in the Food May Day demonstrations, protesting the country's broken food delivery system.

WEDNESDAY MAY 17

Children participating in the protest known as Food May Day for
food supplies in Japan, 1946

THURSDAY MAY 18

NOTES:

FRIDAY MAY 19

SATURDAY MAY 20

SUNDAY MAY 21

_____

_____

_____

_____

_____

_____

_____

_____

MONDAY MAY 22

_____

_____

_____

_____

_____

_____

_____

TUESDAY MAY 23

_____

_____

_____

_____

_____

_____

_____

MAY 21, 1833 William Apess, preacher, politician and descendant of the Wampanoag King Phillip, joins the Mashpee in Massachusetts in revolt against colonial abuses. "I cast my eye upon that white skin, and if I saw those crimes written upon it, I should enter my protest against it immediately and cleave to that which is more honorable."

MAY 21, 1998 Suharto resigns as president of Indonesia after three decades of authoritarian rule. "If proposals are rejected without consideration, voices silenced, criticism banned for no reason, accused of subversion and disturbing the peace, then there is only one word: resist!"
—"WARNING," WHOSE AUTHOR WIJI THUKUL DISAPPEARED AFTER PARTICIPATING IN ANTI-GOVERNMENT PROTESTS IN 1996

MAY 24, 1798 Society of United Irishmen, a republican group influenced by the American and French revolutions, rises up against English rule in what becomes the Irish Rebellion.

"A wet winter, a dry spring
A bloody summer, and no King."
—IRISH SAYING

MAY 25, 1899 Bengal's "rebel poet" Kazi Nazrul Islam is born.

"And I shall rest, battle-weary rebel, only on the day
when the wails of the oppressed shall not rend the air and sky."
—"THE REBEL"

WEDNESDAY MAY 24

Demonstrations and riots against Suharto, May 1998

THURSDAY MAY 25

NOTES:

FRIDAY MAY 26

SATURDAY MAY 27

SUNDAY MAY 28

_____

_____

_____

_____

_____

_____

_____

_____

MONDAY MAY 29

_____

_____

_____

_____

_____

_____

_____

TUESDAY MAY 30

_____

_____

_____

_____

_____

_____

_____

MAY 28, 1913 Six hundred black women march through Bloemfontein, South Africa to protest the law requiring them, as non-white workers, to carry proof of employment.

> "Too long have they submitted
> to white malignity;
> No passes they would carry
> but assert their dignity."
>> —POEM INSPIRED BY THE EVENT, SIGNED "JOHNNY THE OFFICE BOY"

MAY 28, 1918 First Republic of Armenia is declared, following the Armenian Resistance of 1914–18.

MAY 28, 1892 The Sierra Club, which sought to conserve nature and establish national parks, is founded by Scottish-born American John Muir. "Our magnificent redwoods and much of the sugar-pine forests of Sierra Nevada [have] been absorbed by foreign and resident capitalists." —"THE DESTRUCTION OF THE REDWOODS"

MAY 29, 1851 Sojourner Truth, abolitionist speaker, delivers her famous "Ain't I a Woman" speech to the Women's Convention in Akron, Ohio. "I can't read, but I can hear. I have heard the Bible and I learned that Eve caused man to sin. Well, if woman upset the world, do give her a chance to set it right again."

MAY 29, 1963 Peruvian revolutionary Hugo Blanco is captured after leading a "Land or Death" peasant uprising that sparked the country's first agrarian reform. Blanco was spared from execution thanks to pleas from Bertrand Russell, Jean-Paul Sartre, Simone de Beauvoir, Che Guevara, and others. "To be a revolutionary is to love the world, to love life, to be happy." —"TO MY PEOPLE," WRITTEN FROM EL FRONTÓN PENAL COLONY

WEDNESDAY MAY 31

_____

_____

_____

_____

_____

_____

_____

Armenian Revolutionary Federation fighters, banner reading
"Liberty or Death"

THURSDAY JUNE 1

_____

_____

_____

_____

_____

_____

_____

NOTES:

_____

_____

_____

_____

_____

_____

FRIDAY JUNE 2

_____

_____

_____

_____

_____

_____

_____

SATURDAY JUNE 3

_____

_____

_____

_____

_____

_____

_____

BORDERS ARE NEW
GRACIE MAE BRADLEY AND LUKE DE NORONHA

Immigration controls as we know them are a relatively recent innovation. Before the late nineteenth century, controls on mobility—vagrancy laws, for example—tended to focus on preventing people from leaving state territory or restricting their movement within domestic space. In 1882, the US government introduced the Chinese Exclusion Act, prohibiting the immigration of all Chinese labourers, and heralding the beginning of modern controls on immigration. In Canada, immigration controls were introduced at the turn of the twentieth century in response to racist resentment towards Indian immigrant labourers. Meanwhile, the 'White Australia' policy effectively prohibited the immigration of all non-European people to Australia—a policy that was backed by all governments and mainstream parties from the 1890s until the 1950s.

Prior to the introduction of immigration controls, the labour needs of these settler colonies had been served by transatlantic slavery, indenture, and transportation. Indeed,

it was the movement of negatively racialised yet legally free migrants into these territories in the late nineteenth century that seems to have precipitated the introduction of immigration controls. The response to the arrival and settlement of racially undesirable migrants in these settler colonies paved the way for the bordered world we now inhabit.

One way of describing these historical processes is to note that, as states transition from colonial to national forms, they tend to introduce wide-ranging immigration restrictions. This perspective can help us explain the history of British immigration restrictions in the twentieth century, for example. The first immigration restrictions in the UK came with the 1905 Aliens Act, which was explicitly designed to limit the immigration of Jewish migrants escaping persecution in Eastern Europe. But the most significant extension of immigration controls came from 1962 onwards, with the advent of controls on Commonwealth immigrants. After the Second World War, thousands of colonial

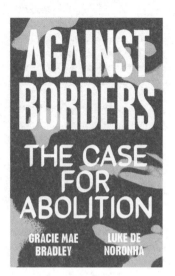

and Commonwealth subjects moved to the UK from the Caribbean, Africa and South Asia. The racist response from politicians, employers and the general public was intense. In this context, the British government introduced immigration and nationality laws that in effect excluded black and brown Commonwealth subjects from any rights of political membership. The UK defined itself as a nation-state, as an island nation, precisely through the exclusion of people from formerly colonised territories, via the introduction of border controls targeting black and brown colonial and Commonwealth migrants.

Bordered nation-states are thus relatively novel political formations that emerged out of long histories of empire, colonialism and slavery. When we recognise that colonialism 'eats into the present', divisions between territories and populations no longer appear so natural and just. Indeed, borders no longer seem ethically defensible. Most nation-states only became independent after the Second World War; previously, they were colonies of European imperial powers, which explains their global marginality and underdevelopment today. Contemporary borders therefore reproduce racial and colonial inequalities, which helps to explain why bordering practices are most intense precisely at the borders between the developed and underdeveloped world: at the edges of Europe and the southern border of the United States.

This is a revised extract from Against Borders: The Case for Abolition *by Gracie Mae Bradley and Luke de Noronha (Verso, 2022).*

SUNDAY JUNE 4

_____

_____

_____

_____

_____

_____

_____

MONDAY JUNE 5

_____

_____

_____

_____

_____

_____

TUESDAY JUNE 6

_____

_____

_____

_____

_____

_____

_____

JUNE 4, 1920 The republican-socialist Jangal movement forms the short-lived Persian Soviet Socialist State in the Gilan province of Iran. "By the will of the working people, Soviet power has been organized in Persia." —LETTER TO TROTSKY FROM THE REVOLUTIONARY WAR COUNCIL OF THE PERSIAN RED ARMY

JUNE 4, 1989 As army tanks roll into Beijing's Tiananmen Square, protestors join Hou Dejian in singing his popular song, "Heirs of the Dragon."

"Enemies on all sides, the sword of the dictator.
For how many years did those gunshots resound?"

JUNE 5, 1940 Novelist and Yorkshire radical J. B. Priestley broadcasts his first "Postscript" radio series for the BBC, which drew audiences of up to 16 million listeners, and was soon cancelled for being too leftist.

JUNE 7, 1903 James Connolly founds the Socialist Labour Party with comrades in Edinburgh; he is later executed for his role in the Easter Uprising. "Before a shot has been fired by the British army on land, before a battle has been fought at sea, ruin and misery are entering the homes of the working people." —"WAR—WHAT IT MEANS TO YOU"

JUNE 10, 1952 Trinidadian historian, novelist and critic C.L.R. James is detained at Ellis Island to await deportation from the US. "The African bruises and breaks himself against his bars in the interests of freedoms wider than his own." —A HISTORY OF NEGRO REVOLT

JUNE 10, 1967 The June 1967 War between Israel and Syria, Jordan, and Egypt ends in Arab defeat.

WEDNESDAY JUNE 7

_____

_____

_____

_____

_____

_____

Trinidadian historian, novelist and critic C.L.R. James

THURSDAY JUNE 8

_____

_____

_____

_____

_____

_____

NOTES:

_____

_____

_____

_____

_____

FRIDAY JUNE 9

_____

_____

_____

_____

_____

_____

SATURDAY JUNE 10

_____

_____

_____

_____

_____

_____

SUNDAY JUNE 11

_____

_____

_____

_____

_____

_____

_____

MONDAY JUNE 12

_____

_____

_____

_____

_____

_____

_____

TUESDAY JUNE 13

_____

_____

_____

_____

_____

_____

JUNE 12, 1917 Founding of the Liberty League, the first organization of the "New Negro Movement" by Hubert Harrison, a black intellectual and labor leader who immigrated to the US from the US Virgin Islands.

JUNE 13, 1971 The *New York Times* publishes the first of the Daniel Ellsberg–leaked Pentagon Papers, which proved that the US government misled the public on the Vietnam War. "If the war was unjust, as I now regarded it, that meant that every Vietnamese killed by Americans or by the proxies we had financed since the 1950s had been killed by us without justification." —SECRETS: A MEMOIR OF VIETNAM AND THE PENTAGON PAPERS

JUNE 15, 1813 Simón Bolívar issues his "Decree of War to the Death" for independence from Spain in Trujillo, Venezuela. "Spaniards and Canarians, count on death, even if indifferent, if you do not actively work in favor of the independence of America. Americans, count on life, even if guilty."

JUNE 16, 1948 The military arm of the Malayan Communist Party fires the first shots of an insurrection against British rule. "Imperialism wants to suppress our struggle for better living conditions with guns and knives and we must answer with more vigorous and larger-scale unified struggle." —EDITORIAL IN PARTY NEWSPAPER MIN SHENG PAO

JUNE 16, 1971 The Polynesian Panther Party is formed in Auckland as a Maori and Pacific Islander civil rights group.

WEDNESDAY JUNE 14

meet the representatives
of the
POLYNESIAN
PANTHER
PARTY
norman tuiasau
will ilolahia

Polynesian Panther Party poster, c. 1973

THURSDAY JUNE 15

NOTES:

FRIDAY JUNE 16

SATURDAY JUNE 17

SUNDAY JUNE 18

_____

_____

_____

_____

_____

_____

MONDAY JUNE 19

_____

_____

_____

_____

_____

_____

TUESDAY JUNE 20

_____

_____

_____

_____

_____

_____

JUNE 18, 1984 British police attack picketing miners with dogs, riot gear and armored vehicles, in a pivotal event of the 1984–85 UK Miners' Strike. The Battle of Orgreave is believed to be the first use of kettling, the police tactic of deploying a large cordon of officers to surround and entrap protesters.

•**JUNE 19, 1977** Ali Shariati, "the ideologue of the Iranian Revolution," is assassinated by the Shah's spies in the UK. "The minds of the people are prepared. The hearts of the enslaved masses are throbbing for revolt under the curtain of secrecy. One spark will be sufficient." —"RED SHI'ISM VS BLACK SHI'ISM"

JUNE 22, 1955 Historian Eric Williams founds the People's National Movement, which later ushers in independence in Trinidad and Tobago. "The history of our West Indian islands can be expressed in two simple words: Columbus and Sugar." —CAPITALISM AND SLAVERY

JUNE 22, 1897 Indian anticolonialists shoot two British officers, and independence leader Bal Gangadhar Tilak is arrested for incitement. "Swaraj [self-rule] is my birthright and I shall have it!"

WEDNESDAY JUNE 21

Ali Shariati on the Haj

THURSDAY JUNE 22

NOTES:

FRIDAY JUNE 23

SATURDAY JUNE 24

SUNDAY JUNE 25

JUNE 25, 1876 Battle of Little Bighorn begins in what is now Montana, with combined Lakota, Cheyenne, and Arapaho forces beating the US 7th Cavalry. "I have robbed, killed, and injured too many white men to believe in a good peace. They are medicine, and I would eventually die a lingering death. I would rather die on the field of battle." —NATIVE LEADER SITTING BULL

JUNE 25, 1892 Ida B. Wells, civil rights activist and anti-lynching campaigner, publishes an early version of her pamphlet "Southern Horrors: Lynch Law in All Its Phases."

MONDAY JUNE 26

JUNE 25, 1962 Mozambique's anticolonial liberation party FRELIMO is founded. In the early 1970s, its guerrilla force of 7,000 fought 60,000 Portuguese colonial troops.

"In our land
bullets are beginning to flower."
—JORGE REBELO, POET BEHIND FRELIMO'S
PROPAGANDA CAMPAIGN

JUNE 27, 1905 The Industrial Workers of the World is founded in Chicago, combining Marxist and trade unionist principles.

JUNE 27, 1880 Helen Keller, world-renowned deafblind author and speaker, is born in Alabama. "If I ever contribute to the Socialist movement the book that I sometimes dream of, I know what I shall name it: Industrial Blindness and Social Deafness." —"HOW I BECAME A SOCIALIST"

TUESDAY JUNE 27

JUNE 28, 1969 Riots begin at New York City's Stonewall Inn in response to a police raid, sparking the modern gay rights movement.

JUNE 30, 1855 The Santhal Rebellion, led by two brothers, sees peasants across the Bengal Presidency rise up against the British Raj and local landlords.

WEDNESDAY JUNE 28

Marsha P. Johnson and Sylvia Rivera, prominent activists who led the Stonewall Riots

THURSDAY JUNE 29

NOTES:

FRIDAY JUNE 30

SATURDAY JULY 1

In Dark Times We Grow Towards the Light by Meredith Stern
(Justseeds Artists' Cooperative/justseeds.org)

Solidarity with Palestine by Roger Peet
(Justseeds Artists' Cooperative/justseeds.org)

SUNDAY JULY 2

_____

_____

_____

_____

_____

_____

_____

MONDAY JULY 3

_____

_____

_____

_____

_____

_____

TUESDAY JULY 4

_____

_____

_____

_____

_____

_____

_____

JULY 2, 1809 Shawnee chief Tecumseh calls on all Indians to unite against the encroachment of white settlers on native land. "The only way to stop this evil is for all the red men to unite in claiming an equal right in the land. That is how it was at first, and should be still, for the land never was divided, but was for the use of everyone." —ADDRESS TO WILLIAM HENRY HARRISON

JULY 4, 1789 The Marquis de Sade is moved from the Bastille prison to Charenton, days before French revolutionaries storm it and set fire to his writings there. "No act of possession can ever be perpetrated on a free being; it is as unjust to own a wife monogamously as it is to own slaves." —"PHILOSOPHY IN THE BEDROOM"

JULY 4, 1876 Susan B. Anthony and other protesters present the "Declaration of Rights for Women" at an official celebration of the centennial of the United States. "Women's wealth, thought, and labor have cemented the stones of every monument man has reared to liberty."

JULY 4, 1967 The British Parliament decriminalizes homosexuality.

JULY 5, 1885 The Protect the King movement in Vietnam begins, following a French attack on the imperial capital of Hue, and uniting the country against French colonial rule. "Better to be sentenced once than sentenced for eternity." —COORDINATOR OF RESISTANCE IN NORTHERN VIETNAM NGUYỄN QUANG BÍCH, LETTER TO THE FRENCH

JULY 7, 1969 Redstockings, a New York–based radical Marxist-feminist group, publishes its manifesto. "Liberated women—very different from women's liberation!" —REDSTOCKINGS MEMBER PAT MAINARDI, "THE POLITICS OF HOUSEWORK"

WEDNESDAY JULY 5

Design proposal for a US dollar featuring Susan B. Anthony,
1978–79

THURSDAY JULY 6

NOTES:

FRIDAY JULY 7

SATURDAY JULY 8

SUNDAY JULY 9

_____

_____

_____

_____

_____

_____

MONDAY JULY 10

_____

_____

_____

_____

_____

TUESDAY JULY 11

_____

_____

_____

_____

_____

JULY 9, 1910 Govan Mbeki, leader of the South African Communist Party and the African National Congress, born. Following the Rivonia Trial, Mbeki served a long-term on Robben Island, during which he managed to run education classes with prisoners, many on Marxist theory, and wrote a number of significant analyses from jail.

JULY 13, 1524 Thomas Müntzer, radical German theologian who became a leader in the Peasants' War of 1524 to 1525, delivers his famous "Sermon to the Princes" to Saxon nobles. "Oh, you beloved lords, how well the Lord will smash down the old pots of clay [ecclesiastical authorities] with his rod of iron."

JULY 13, 1934 Nobel Prize–winning Nigerian poet and playwright Wole Soyinka is born. Over the course of his life, Soyinka is prosecuted and jailed numerous times for his outspoken political critiques.

"Traveler you must set forth
At dawn.
I promise marvels of the holy hour."
—"DEATH IN THE DAWN"

JULY 14, 1789 An organized mob breaks into a royal armory in Paris and, newly armed, storms the Bastille, a fortress that held the monarchy's political prisoners. "This very night all the Swiss and German battalions will leave the Champ de Mars to massacre us all. One resource is left; to take arms!" —SPEECH BY JOURNALIST CAMILLE DESMOU-LINS THAT ROUSED THE PEOPLE THE PREVIOUS DAY

JULY 14, 1877 The Great Railroad Strike begins in West Virginia, United States, pitting thousands of railroad workers against state militias and the national guardsmen summoned to break it. "Wages and revenge." —SLOGAN

WEDNESDAY JULY 12

_____

_____

_____

_____

_____

_____

_____

Activists and supporters march outside the Rivonia Trial, 1964

THURSDAY JULY 13

_____

_____

_____

_____

_____

_____

_____

NOTES:

_____

_____

_____

_____

_____

_____

FRIDAY JULY 14

_____

_____

_____

_____

_____

_____

SATURDAY JULY 15

_____

_____

_____

_____

_____

_____

SUNDAY JULY 16

_____

_____

_____

_____

_____

_____

_____

MONDAY JULY 17

_____

_____

_____

_____

_____

_____

_____

TUESDAY JULY 18

_____

_____

_____

_____

_____

_____

_____

JULY 18, 1936 Resistance fighter Buenaventura Durruti forms the "Durruti Column," the largest anarchist fighting force in the Spanish Civil War. "The bourgeoisie might blast and ruin its own world before it leaves the stage of history. We carry a new world here, in our hearts." —DURRUTI IN AN INTERVIEW THREE MONTHS BEFORE BEING KILLED

JULY 19, 1961 The Sandinista National Liberation Front (FSLN) is founded; in 1979 it will overthrow the Somoza dictatorship in Nicaragua. "Those of us who propose to wage a struggle to liberate our country and make freedom a reality must rescue our own traditions and put together the facts and figures we need in order to wage an ideological war against our enemy." —FSLN COFOUNDER CARLOS FONSECA, SPEECH IN HAVANA

JULY 19, 1979 Ernesto Cardenal, Liberation Theology priest and poet aligned with the Sandinistas, becomes the first minister of culture under the new revolutionary government.

"We shall celebrate in the great squares the anniversary of the Revolution
The God that does exist is the god of the workers."

—PSALM ("SALMO") 43

JULY 20, 1925 Frantz Fanon, psychiatrist and revolutionary whose writings inspired anticolonial movements throughout the world, is born in Martinique. "HISTORY teaches us clearly that the battle against colonialism does not run straight away along the lines of nationalism." —THE WRETCHED OF THE EARTH

WEDNESDAY JULY 19

Sandinistas taking a smoke break, 1987

THURSDAY JULY 20

NOTES:

FRIDAY JULY 21

SATURDAY JULY 22

SUNDAY JULY 23

_____

_____

_____

_____

_____

_____

_____

MONDAY JULY 24

_____

_____

_____

_____

_____

_____

_____

TUESDAY JULY 25

_____

_____

_____

_____

_____

_____

_____

JULY 23, 1900 W. E. B. Du Bois attends the First Pan-African Congress in London, where he makes the statement later immortalized in his 1903 book _Souls of Black Folk_: "The problem of the twentieth century is the problem of the color-line."

JULY 25, 1846 Henry David Thoreau is jailed for refusing to pay taxes due to his opposition to slavery and the Mexican-American war. "Under a government which imprisons any unjustly, the true place for a just man is also a prison." —_CIVIL DISOBEDIENCE_

JULY 26, 1953 Fidel Castro leads the Cuban revolution against the US-backed dictator Fulgencio Batista with an attack on the Moncada Barracks. "Condemn me. It does not matter. History will absolve me." —CASTRO, BEFORE BEING SENTENCED FOR THE ATTACK

JULY 26, 1956 Gamal Abdel Nasser, president of Egypt, announces the nationalization of the Suez Canal. "We shall yield neither to force nor the dollar."

JULY 27, 1972 Selma James, cofounder of the International Wages for Housework campaign, and Mariarosa Dalla Costa publish _The Power of Women and the Subversion of the Community_, which identified women's unwaged care work as an essential element of capitalism.

JULY 28, 1794 Maximilien Robespierre, the face of the French Revolution's Reign of Terror, is guillotined without a trial. "The tyrant's trial is insurrection; his judgment is the fall of his power; his penalty, whatever the liberty of the people demands." —"AGAINST GRANTING THE KING A TRIAL"

JULY 29, 1848 The Young Irelander Rebellion of 1848 takes place: a failed Irish nationalist revolt against British rule, sometimes called the Famine Rebellion (since it took place during the Great Irish Famine) or the Battle of Ballingarry.

WEDNESDAY JULY 26

W. E. B. Du Bois—American sociologist, historian, civil rights
activist, Pan-Africanist, author and editor—in 1918

THURSDAY JULY 27

NOTES:

FRIDAY JULY 28

SATURDAY JULY 29

I FEAR MY PAIN INTERESTS YOU
STEPHANIE LACAVA

That day, I counted the cows. One two three four five six seven eight. I couldn't find the ninth, and wondered if she too had vanished. There was a break in the electric wire, as if someone had bent the top line one way and the bottom the other. No cow could have gotten through—not even a crow, which explained the iridescent hash on the ground, scalped beak-skull. Josephine said a group of crows was called a murder. I used my foot to grind the remains deeper into the mulch. No spark, no glitter left in the soil.

I heard a sound behind me.

No one was there. No Eight or even Nine. I knew what I was going to do, though I kept telling myself in my head not to do it. Be careful. Remember the fried crow: lit up, ashes of black opal, fat carcass in the grass. I had come close before and what had held me back wasn't a sensation, but a feeling. Two different things. I didn't know they weren't the same then. Somewhere the feeling said not to. It warned my brain based on hammered-in information, notably Josephine telling me, "Stay away from the herd." In my mind, this also meant the wire links. Words can get mixed up and are difficult to unravel when you don't have sensation. I felt plugged, trapped, unable to release something I couldn't explain. Josephine had sensed it that morning as she questioned me. "What will you do today?"

"I don't know."

"Why don't you sit on the porch and paint."

"I feel heavy."

"Heavy? You weigh one hundred pounds. Please don't start."

"No, it's not a physical thing." I couldn't explain that it wasn't physical in the second sense, but also not about my body.

"I will set up the materials. You will get dressed. Then come down to paint. Or do you want to go into your grandfather's studio?"

"To paint?"

"Certainly not to play the guitar?"

"How do you know?"

"Watch your tone, young lady."

"I take lessons."

"You do?"

"Yes, from my father."

"Not the greatest guitar player in the world."

"Right, he's ranked twenty-fifth."

"See?"

"You're hopeless."

"Your mother is a better musician."

"You think she's a better everything."

"You're hers, too." It was a strange thing for a grandmother to say. I didn't know if she meant that I was more valuable as my mother's daughter than my father's, or that my value was in belonging at one remove to Josephine. It was painful to sit there trying to decode her riddles as she stared at me. Always a palpable smugness, her chin lifted the tiniest bit too high, so she could look down her perfect little nose.

"Gotta go," I said, without waiting for a response.

It took three minutes to get to the field that morning. In the past when I had timed it on my phone, it was always five or seven. But that day I ran, full of determination. Josephine had not yelled after me. She didn't yell. Ever. That was only for people who were out of control. She was always performing being a human being to her own playbook.

I walked to the break in the fence and placed one palm on each end of the cut wire.

At first I felt nothing. And then came a shiver, like when I would play with my mother's friend's daughter's hair. She and her friends were always playing strange games that let you touch one another in acceptable ways, to create sensations that were not.

That chill. Then, nothing.

And then another shiver, this time in my legs. My feet were always numb, even on the hot sand in summer beyond the touch of the tide. Or when my father, almost drunk, on one of his nights would make me run barefoot in the city snow. I felt nothing then. He would lift his feet like sewing machine pins and they would turn bright pink. I felt nothing. Told no one.

This is a revised extract from I Fear My Pain Interests You *by Stephanie LaCava (Verso, 2022).*

SUNDAY JULY 30

_____

_____

_____

_____

_____

_____

_____

MONDAY JULY 31

_____

_____

_____

_____

_____

_____

TUESDAY AUGUST 1

_____

_____

_____

_____

_____

_____

JULY 31, 1905 The Maji Maji rebellion begins in what is now Tanzania, led by several tribes in Tanganyika against German colonizers. "Hongo or the European, which is the stronger?" "Hongo!" —REBELLION PASSWORD

AUGUST 1, 1933 Anti-Fascist activists Bruno Tesch, Walter Möller, Karl Wolff and August Lütgens executed by the Nazi regime in Altona.

AUGUST 2, 1924 James Baldwin, black American novelist, critic, and essayist, is born in Harlem, New York City. "People can cry much easier than they can change, a rule of psychology people like me picked up as kids on the street." —"JAMES BALDWIN BACK HOME"

AUGUST 2, 1997 Fela Kuti, Nigerian father of Afrobeat and frequent presidential candidate, dies from AIDS-related complications.

AUGUST 3, 1960 Independence Day in the Republic of Niger, marking the nation's independence from France in 1960. Since 1975, it is also Arbor Day, as trees are planted across the nation to aid the fight against desertification.

AUGUST 4, 1983 Revolutionary leader Thomas Sankara assumes power in Burkina Faso, nationalizing mineral wealth and redistributing land. "It took the madmen of yesterday for us to be able to act with extreme clarity today. I want to be one of those madmen. We must dare to invent the future."

AUGUST 5, 1951 Eduardo Chibas, anti-communist Cuban radio personality, shoots himself after his final broadcast. "People of Cuba, keep awake. This is my last knock at your door." —CHIBAS'S LAST WORDS

WEDNESDAY AUGUST 2

Writer and critic James Baldwin (1924–1987)

THURSDAY AUGUST 3

NOTES:

FRIDAY AUGUST 4

SATURDAY AUGUST 5

SUNDAY AUGUST 6

_____

_____

_____

_____

_____

_____

MONDAY AUGUST 7

_____

_____

_____

_____

_____

_____

TUESDAY AUGUST 8

_____

_____

_____

_____

_____

_____

_____

AUGUST 6, 1969 Theodor Adorno—philosopher, composer and leading member of the Frankfurt School of critical theory—dies. "For the Enlightenment, anything which cannot be resolved into numbers, and ultimately into one, is illusion; modern positivism consigns it to poetry." —DIALECTIC OF ENLIGHTENMENT, CO-AUTHORED WITH MAX HORKHEIMER

AUGUST 6, 2011 Riots break out throughout London after police kill a black man, lasting for several days and leading to more than 3,000 arrests.

AUGUST 8, 1961 Wu Han, a member of a dissident group of Chinese intellectuals, writes a play indirectly critical of Mao and the Great Leap Forward, for which he is imprisoned.

> "You pay lip service to the principle
> that the people are the roots of the state.
> But officials still oppress the masses
> while pretending to be virtuous men."
> —"HAI JUI'S DISMISSAL"

AUGUST 8, 1988 Rangoon students call openly for democracy, sparking the 8888 Uprising that toppled Burma's Ne Win government before being violently crushed by government troops.

AUGUST 9, 1650 The English Parliament passes an act outlawing "blasphemous" sects like the Ranters, one of the most radical to emerge during the English Revolution, which denied the authority of churches, priests, and writ.

AUGUST 11, 1828 The first Working Men's Party of the United States is founded in Philadelphia. "And for the support of this declaration, we mutually pledge to each other our faithful aid to the end of our lives." —GEORGE HENRY EVANS, "PARTY DECLARATION OF INDEPENDENCE"

WEDNESDAY AUGUST 9

Shop fire in Clapham Junction during the London Riots, August 8, 2011

THURSDAY AUGUST 10

NOTES:

FRIDAY AUGUST 11

SATURDAY AUGUST 12

SUNDAY AUGUST 13

MONDAY AUGUST 14

TUESDAY AUGUST 15

AUGUST 14, 1980 Polish shipyard workers strike to protest the firing of worker Anna Walentynowicz and for the right to form unions. Walentynowicz is reinstated, and several weeks later, the first independent labor union in a Soviet bloc country, Solidarność, is formed, precipitating the fall of the Polish communist regime. "It was the end of the utopian dream, and it enabled us to dismantle the dictatorship by negotiation." —ACTIVIST ADAM MICHNIK

AUGUST 15, 1947 India becomes independent after 200 years of British colonial rule. "A moment comes, which comes but rarely in history, when we step out from the old to the new, when an age ends, and when the soul of a nation, long suppressed, finds utterance." —MOVEMENT LEADER AND INDIA'S FIRST PRIME MINISTER JAWAHARLAL NEHRU, "TRYST WITH DESTINY"

AUGUST 16, 1819 The English cavalry charges into a crowd of over 60,000 rallying in Manchester for parliamentary reform in what becomes known as the Peterloo Massacre.

"Rise like lions after slumber
In unvanquishable number!
Shake your chains to earth like dew
Which in sleep had fallen on you:
Ye are many—they are few!"

—PERCY BYSSHE SHELLEY'S "THE MASQUE OF ANARCHY,"
AN EARLY STATEMENT OF NONVIOLENT RESISTANCE

AUGUST 19, 1953 Mohammad Mosaddegh, the popular, democratically elected prime minister of Iran, is overthrown by a CIA-backed coup. "My greatest sin is that I nationalized Iran's oil industry and discarded the system of political and economic exploitation by the world's greatest empire." —SPEECH AT HIS TRIAL

WEDNESDAY AUGUST 16

A painting of the Peterloo Massacre circulated in pro-suffrage papers, 1819

THURSDAY AUGUST 17

NOTES:

FRIDAY AUGUST 18

SATURDAY AUGUST 19

SUNDAY AUGUST 20

MONDAY AUGUST 21

TUESDAY AUGUST 22

AUGUST 21, 1791 A rebellion against slavery breaks out in Saint Domingue, leading to the Haitian Revolution, the only slave revolt against European colonialists that successfully achieved an independent state. "We seek only to bring men to the liberty that God has given them, and that other men have taken from them only by transgressing His immutable will." —REVOLUTIONARY LEADER TOUSSAINT L'OUVERTURE

AUGUST 21, 1940 Leon Trotsky, Marxist revolutionary and theorist, is assassinated by Soviet agents. "Life is beautiful. Let the future generations cleanse it of all evil, oppression and violence, and enjoy it to the full." —"TROTSKY'S TESTAMENT," WRITTEN MONTHS EARLIER

AUGUST 23, 1927 During the Red Scare—a period of intense political repression in the US—the Italian-born anarchists Nicola Sacco and Bartolomeo Vanzetti are wrongfully convicted and executed for robbery and murder.

AUGUST 25, 1968 Yippies—the Youth International Party, which brought counterculture theatricality to the US antiwar and New Left movements—host their Festival of Life at the Democratic National Convention in Chicago, leading to police actions and a trial for conspiracy to riot for the organizers. "There will be public fornication whenever and wherever there is an aroused appendage and willing apertures." —ACTIVIST ED SANDERS, "PREDICTIONS FOR YIPPIE ACTIVITIES"

AUGUST 26 1789 The "Declaration of the Rights of Man and of the Citizen"—a document of the French Revolution and civil rights—is adopted by the National Constituent Assembly in France.

WEDNESDAY AUGUST 23

Declaration of the Rights of Man and of the Citizen, painted by Jean-Jacques-François Le Barbier

THURSDAY AUGUST 24

NOTES:

FRIDAY AUGUST 25

SATURDAY AUGUST 26

SUNDAY AUGUST 27

_____

_____

_____

_____

_____

_____

_____

MONDAY AUGUST 28

_____

_____

_____

_____

_____

_____

TUESDAY AUGUST 29

_____

_____

_____

_____

_____

_____

AUGUST 29, 1786 Poor farmers crushed by debt and taxes rise up in armed rebellion in Massachusetts, US, in what came to be known as Shay's Rebellion. "The great men are going to get all we have and I think it is time for us to rise and put a stop to it, and have no more courts, nor sheriffs, nor collectors, nor lawyers." —PLOUGH JOGGER, FARMER, SPEAKING AT THE ILLEGAL CONVENTION OPPOSING THE MASSACHUSETTS LEGISLATURE

AUGUST 29, 1844 Edward Carpenter, pioneering socialist poet, philosopher, and early homosexual thinker, is born in England. "It has become clear that the number of individuals affected with 'sexual inversion' in some degree or other is very great—much greater than is generally supposed to be the case." —HOMOGENIC LOVE

SEPTEMBER 1, 1961 The Eritrean struggle for independence begins when members of the Eritrean Liberation Front fire first shots on the occupying Ethiopian army.

> "What have I done
> That you deny me my torch?"
> —"SHIGEY HABUNI," POPULAR SONG WITH TIES TO THE NATIONALIST MOVEMENT

SEPTEMBER 2, 1872 Russian revolutionary and anarchist theorist Mikhail Bakunin is expelled from the First International, presaging a split between the anarchist and Marxist factions of the workers' movement.

SEPTEMBER 2, 1945 Following two weeks of insurgency against French colonial forces, Ho Chi Minh and the Viet Minh seize control of the country and declare Vietnam independent. "Poor Indochina! You will die, if your old-fashioned youth do not resuscitate themselves." —HO CHI MINH PAMPHLET THAT BECAME THE "BIBLE OF NATIONALISTS" TWO DECADES LATER

WEDNESDAY AUGUST 30

_____

_____

_____

_____

_____

_____

_____

Ho Chi Minh (1890–1969) with East German sailors in Stralsund
Harbor, 1957

THURSDAY AUGUST 31

_____

_____

_____

_____

_____

_____

_____

NOTES:

_____

_____

_____

_____

_____

_____

FRIDAY SEPTEMBER 1

_____

_____

_____

_____

_____

_____

_____

SATURDAY SEPTEMBER 2

_____

_____

_____

_____

_____

_____

THE DEATH (AND LIFE) OF HOMOSEXUALITY
HUW LEMMEY AND BEN MILLER

Is it not time we also look at those whom the early gay rights pioneers were less keen to claim as *family*, as *one of us*? Or the people among those pioneers—the people who helped bake the cake of identity and desire that now defines our lives—who perhaps irreparably harmed the substance of 'gay' itself? Within their lives, buffeted by the winds of history and social circumstance, many same-sex-loving and gender non-conforming chose terrible paths and inflicted appalling damage upon others.

If we are to accept that some of the greatest artists, activists, and poets of history were guided and motivated by their sexuality, why not the criminals, despots, and bigots? Within their lives are valuable lessons regarding how we came to understand ourselves, about the challenges LGBTQ people have faced—not always honourably—through history, and how sex, love, and desire have led people to make world-changing decisions. It is not simply that these are fascinating, complex lives that compel us towards understanding homosexuality.

They also ask us to pose the question of the whole notion of gay heroes: why do we choose to remember, and why do we choose to forget?

When a gay man becomes a fascist, how does his homosexuality affect his attraction to the politics of venerating the state as though it were a go-go boy dancing on a box? When a king takes young male lovers and is then blackmailed, and when the process of forcing peasants off their land is tied to the same moral opprobrium that threatens the king, what are the transactions of power and influence at play? When a bisexual anthropologist relies on primitivist projections of colonized Others to find answers for how she might live now, in a society that sees her queerness as terrifying and backwards and a threat to the modern, how might her desires have affected the mythic nostalgia of her work and thus the course of twentieth-century anthropological thinking? Why do configurations of identity and desire that seem to have expired continue to hold such power over so many people, including us, the authors? Why can't we finally kill or abandon homosexuality and do something else, something better, instead?

Ultimately, this book is a project of demystification and an act of love. 'Gay is good,' went the old slogan, but it's no good at all on its own. As you will see, many of the queers with the very worst political goals have wanted to position themselves as heirs to a secret or magical kingdom, as the inheritors of a chain of heroes. The process of making the movement and the identity has often involved reifying, recreating, and worshipping power and evil in their most brute forms. Maybe it is time that homosexuality itself dies, that we find new and more functional and more appropriate configurations for our politics and desires. Or maybe being queer is just as transitory and incomplete as anything else. Maybe all of us are lost and scared, subject to forces beyond our control, and trying to figure out how to configure our unruly desires and our politics into an ethical way of being in the world.

If there is anything of homosexuality to be saved, it is its reconstruction of the concept of the family. Not born into fixed kin, we get to choose ours. This is a project of socialization but also of politicization, of understanding to which kind of political 'we' we wish to belong. Understanding how we became a 'we' in the first place—and interrogating the extent to which that 'we' even makes sense, given how different 'we' have been from one another and how terribly 'we' have often been treated by one another—might help more of us choose better. Then the real work begins.

This is a revised extract from Bad Gays: A Homosexual History *by Huw Lemmey and Ben Miller (Verso, 2022).*

SUNDAY SEPTEMBER 3

_____

_____

_____

_____

_____

_____

_____

MONDAY SEPTEMBER 4

_____

_____

_____

_____

_____

_____

TUESDAY SEPTEMBER 5

_____

_____

_____

_____

_____

_____

_____

SEPTEMBER 3, 2017 Private security guards for the Dakota Access Pipeline unleash dogs on indigenous water protectors near the Standing Rock Sioux Tribe reservation in North Dakota. A protest encampment, established months earlier, quickly swelled to become the largest gathering of Native Americans in recent history. "Mní Wičoni—Water is Life." —SLOGAN

SEPTEMBER 6, 1960 "Manifesto of the 121" is signed by French intellectuals (including Jean-Paul Sartre, Maurice Blanchot, and others), supporting the right of Algerians to fight for independence from the French. "Must we be reminded that fifteen years after the destruction of the Hitlerite order, French militarism has managed to bring back torture and restore it as an institution in Europe?"

SEPTEMBER 8, 1965 Delano Grape Strike begins in California when Filipino grape pickers walk out and ask Cesar Chavez, leader of the mostly Latino National Farm Workers Association, to join them. The campaign ended five years later in success, largely due to a consumer boycott. "Time accomplishes for the poor what money does for the rich." —CHAVEZ, "LETTER FROM DELANO"

SEPTEMBER 9, 869 Ali ibn Muhammad, a leader of the Zanj uprising of African slaves against the Abbasid Caliphate in Iraq, begins freeing slaves and gaining adherents. "Ali ordered their slaves to bring whips of palm branches and, while their masters and agents were prostrated on the ground, each one was given five hundred lashes." —PERSIAN HISTORIAN IBN JARIR AL-TABARI

SEPTEMBER 9, 1739 Stono Rebellion, the largest slave uprising in Britain's mainland North American colonies, led by a slave called Jemmy, erupts near Charleston, South Carolina. Over the next two years, slave uprisings occurred independently in Georgia and South Carolina.

WEDNESDAY SEPTEMBER 6

Cesar Chavez (1927–1993) following the successful farmworker strike and consumer grape boycott, 1970

THURSDAY SEPTEMBER 7

NOTES:

FRIDAY SEPTEMBER 8

SATURDAY SEPTEMBER 9

SUNDAY SEPTEMBER 10

_____

_____

_____

_____

_____

_____

_____

MONDAY SEPTEMBER 11

_____

_____

_____

_____

_____

_____

_____

TUESDAY SEPTEMBER 12

_____

_____

_____

_____

_____

_____

SEPTEMBER 14, 1791 Olympe de Gouges publishes the *Declaration of the Rights of Women and the Female Citizen,* one of the first tracts to champion women's rights. "Woman is born free and remains the equal of man in rights."

SEPTEMBER 15, 1889 Claude McKay, Harlem Renaissance poet and delegate to the Third International, is born in Jamaica.

"If we must die—O let us nobly die!
So that our precious blood may not be shed
In vain; then even the monsters we defy
Shall be constrained to honor us though dead!"

—"IF WE MUST DIE"

SEPTEMBER 16, 1810 Miguel Hidalgo, a priest in Dolores, Mexico, issues a call to revolt against Spanish rule, setting in motion the Mexican War of Independence. "My children: a new dispensation come to us today. Will you receive it? Will you free yourselves?"

SEPTEMBER 16, 1923 Alongside her lover and his six-year-old nephew, Ito Noe, anarchist and feminist writer and activist, is brutally murdered by Japanese police. The event, known as the Amakasu Incident, sparked outrage throughout Japan and led to a ten-year sentence for the officer.

SEPTEMBER 16, 1973 Victor Jara, Chilean poet and songwriter, is tortured and killed in Chile Stadium following Pinochet's coup against Allende.

"How hard is it to sing
when I must sing of horror"

—"ESTADIO CHILE," WRITTEN BY JARA IN THE STADIUM
AND SMUGGLED OUT INSIDE A SHOE

WEDNESDAY SEPTEMBER 13

Ito Noe, Japanese anarchist and feminist

THURSDAY SEPTEMBER 14

NOTES:

FRIDAY SEPTEMBER 15

SATURDAY SEPTEMBER 16

_____

_____

_____

_____

_____

_____

_____

_____

_____

_____

_____

_____

_____

_____

_____

_____

_____

_____

_____

_____

_____

SEPTEMBER 19, 1921 The Brazilian educator and philosopher Paulo Freire is born. His _Pedagogy of the Oppressed_ infuses a classical theory of education with Marxist and anticolonialist approaches. "This, then, is the great humanistic and historical task of the oppressed: to liberate themselves and their oppressors as well."

SEPTEMBER 21, 1956 Nicaraguan poet Rigoberto López Pérez assassinates Anastasio Somoza García, the longtime dictator of Nicaragua, before being killed himself. "Seeing that all efforts to return Nicaragua to being (or to becoming for the first time) a free country without shame or stain have been futile, I have decided that I should be the one to try to initiate the beginning of the end of this tyranny." —LETTER TO HIS MOTHER

SEPTEMBER 23, 1884 Liberal party partisans occupy a mountaintop in Kabasan, Japan, in a rebellion against the Meiji government.

> "Yet while we lament, asking
> why our insignificant selves
> were oppressed,
> the rain still falls
> heavily on the people."
> —PARTICIPANT OHASHI GENZABURO

SEPTEMBER 23, 1973 Pablo Neruda, Chilean poet and Nobel Prize–winner, is poisoned by Pinochet's regime and dies. "When the trumpet blared everything on earth was prepared and Jehovah distributed the world to Coca-Cola Inc., Anaconda, Ford Motors and other entities: the United Fruit Inc. reserved for itself the juiciest, the central seaboard of my land, America's sweet waist." —"UNITED FRUIT CO."

WEDNESDAY SEPTEMBER 20

_____

_____

_____

_____

_____

_____

_____

Neruda (1904–1973) recording his poetry at the US Library of Congress in 1966

THURSDAY SEPTEMBER 21

_____

_____

_____

_____

_____

_____

_____

NOTES:

_____

_____

_____

_____

_____

FRIDAY SEPTEMBER 22

_____

_____

_____

_____

_____

_____

_____

SATURDAY SEPTEMBER 23

_____

_____

_____

_____

_____

_____

SUNDAY SEPTEMBER 24

_____

_____

_____

_____

_____

_____

_____

MONDAY SEPTEMBER 25

_____

_____

_____

_____

_____

_____

_____

TUESDAY SEPTEMBER 26

_____

_____

_____

_____

_____

_____

_____

SEPTEMBER 24, 1838 A meeting held on Kersal Moor in England launches the Chartist movement, the first mass working-class movement in Europe.

SEPTEMBER 26, 1940 Fleeing Vichy France, Marxist theorist Walter Benjamin is threatened with deportation from Spain and kills himself with morphine tablets.

SEPTEMBER 28, 1829 David Walker, a contributor to the first African-American newspaper _Freedom Journal_, publishes his "Appeal to the Colored Citizens of the World," calling for slaves to revolt against their masters. Southern plantation owners respond by putting a $3,000 bounty on his head. "The whites want slaves, and want us for their slaves, but some of them will curse the day they ever saw us."

SEPTEMBER 1875 Senator William Allison arrives in Sioux country to negotiate a land lease agreement with the Native Americans that would have allowed the United States government to mine the area for gold. His proposal is met with 300 mounted warriors, led by Little Big Man, who chant the song below in response.

"The Black Hills is my land and I love it
And whoever interferes
Will hear this gun."
—SIOUX WARRIORS' SONG

SEPTEMBER 30, 1935 The anti-Stalinist Workers' Party of Marxist Unification (POUM) is founded in Spain, where it is especially active during the Civil War. "The totalitarian states can do great things, but there is one thing they cannot do: they cannot give the factory-worker a rifle and tell him to take it home and keep it in his bedroom. That rifle hanging on the wall of the working-class flat or laborer's cottage is the symbol of democracy."
—POUM MEMBER GEORGE ORWELL, ARTICLE IN THE _EVENING STANDARD_

WEDNESDAY SEPTEMBER 27

Great Chartist Meeting on Kennington Common, London in 1848

THURSDAY SEPTEMBER 28

NOTES:

FRIDAY SEPTEMBER 29

SATURDAY SEPTEMBER 30

The Tides are Turning by Sarah Farahat (سارة فرحات)
(Justseeds Artists' Cooperative and the Dissenters / justseeds.org/portfolio/de-mil-i-ta-rise)

Fire Clears the Way by Erik Ruin (erikruin.info)

SUNDAY OCTOBER 1

_____

_____

_____

_____

_____

_____

_____

MONDAY OCTOBER 2

_____

_____

_____

_____

_____

_____

TUESDAY OCTOBER 3

_____

_____

_____

_____

_____

_____

OCTOBER 1, 1949 Mao Zedong establishes the People's Republic of China. "A revolution is not a dinner party, or writing an essay, or painting a picture, or doing embroidery; it cannot be so refined, so leisurely and gentle, so temperate, kind, courteous, restrained and magnanimous." —"REPORT ON AN INVESTIGATION OF THE PEASANT MOVEMENT IN HUNAN"

OCTOBER 5, 1877 Nez Perce leader Hinmatóowy-alahtq'it, also known as Chief Joseph, ends a legendary three-month flight to Canada by surrendering to US forces. "Do not misunderstand me, but understand fully with reference to my affection for the land. I never said the land was mine to do with as I choose. The one who has a right to dispose of it is the one who created it." —"AN INDIAN'S VIEW OF INDIAN AFFAIRS"

OCTOBER 5, 1959 Robert F. Williams's Black Armed Guard fires on Ku Klux Klan members riding past a member's house in North Carolina. "Nowhere in the annals of history does the record show a people delivered from bondage by patience alone." —"WE MUST FIGHT BACK"

OCTOBER 6, 1985 Riots break out on the Broadwater Farm estate in one of London's poorest neighborhoods, a day after an Afro-Caribbean woman died of heart failure during a police search. One police officer was killed.

OCTOBER 7, 1979 Landless farmers occupy the Macali land in Ronda Alta, Brazil, leading to the founding of the Landless Workers Movement (MST). "This is what I've always wanted: 'to overcome, to overcome.'" —MST LEADER MIGUEL ALVES DOS SANTOS

WEDNESDAY OCTOBER 4

FBI "Wanted" poster for civil rights activist Robert F. Williams
(1925–1996)

THURSDAY OCTOBER 5

NOTES:

FRIDAY OCTOBER 6

SATURDAY OCTOBER 7

SUNDAY OCTOBER 8

_____

_____

_____

_____

_____

_____

_____

MONDAY OCTOBER 9

_____

_____

_____

_____

_____

_____

_____

TUESDAY OCTOBER 10

_____

_____

_____

_____

_____

_____

_____

OCTOBER 8, 1969 The Weather Underground, a faction of the Students for a Democratic Society, stages the first of its "Days of Rage," a series of confrontations with the Chicago police in 1969. "Freaks are revolutionaries and revolutionaries are freaks. If you want to find us, this is where we are." —"COMMUNIQUÉ #1"

OCTOBER 10, 1837 Charles Fourier, French utopian socialist credited with inventing the word "feminism," dies after laying out his concept of utopian communities. "The extension of women's rights is the basic principle of all social progress." —THE THEORY OF THE FOUR MOVEMENTS AND THE GENERAL DESTINIES"

OCTOBER 10, 1903 British activist Emmeline Pankhurst cofounds the Women's Social and Political Union, a militant all-women suffragist organization dedicated to "deeds, not words." "The moving spirit of militancy is deep and abiding reverence for human life." —MY OWN STORY

OCTOBER 10, 1911 The Wuchang Uprising begins after the Qing government suppresses political protest against the handover of local railways to foreign ventures. Quickly spreading through China, the Xinhai Revolution took down the 2,100-year-old dynastic empire within months.

OCTOBER 10, 1947 Senegalese railway workers begin a strike that lasted months, in what would become a watershed moment in Senegal's anticolonial struggle. "It rolled out over its own length, like the movement of a serpent. It was as long as a life." —GOD'S BITS OF WOOD, A NOVEL BY FILMMAKER, WRITER, AND ACTIVIST OUSMANE SEMBÈNE BASED ON THE STRIKE

WEDNESDAY OCTOBER 11

The two flags of the Wuchang Uprising at the birth of the Republic of China

THURSDAY OCTOBER 12

NOTES:

FRIDAY OCTOBER 13

SATURDAY OCTOBER 14

SUNDAY OCTOBER 15

_____

_____

_____

_____

_____

_____

_____

MONDAY OCTOBER 16

_____

_____

_____

_____

_____

_____

_____

TUESDAY OCTOBER 17

_____

_____

_____

_____

_____

_____

_____

OCTOBER 15, 1966 The Black Panther Party is founded in Oakland, California. "The people make revolution; the oppressors, by their brutal actions, cause resistance by the people. The vanguard party only teaches the correct methods of resistance." —COFOUNDER HUEY P. NEWTON, "THE CORRECT HANDLING OF A REVOLUTION"

OCTOBER 15, 1968 The Jamaican government bans the Guyanese scholar and Black Power activist Walter Rodney from the country, sparking what became known as the Rodney Riots. "The only great men among the unfree and the oppressed are those who struggle to destroy the oppressor." —HOW EUROPE UNDERDEVELOPED AFRICA

OCTOBER 17, 1961 Algerian demonstrators in Paris, denouncing France's colonial war in their home country, are met with force. An estimated 300 were massacred; the French government acknowledges forty victims.

OCTOBER 18, 1899 The Battle of Senluo Temple breaks out in northern China between government forces and the Militia United in Righteousness—known in English as the "Boxers" for their strict martial arts regimen—in what would eventually become the Boxer Rebellion, an anti-foreign and anti-Christian uprising.

OCTOBER 19, 1986 Samora Machel, Mozambican revolutionary leader and post-independence president, dies in a plane crash in South Africa.

OCTOBER 21, 1956 Dedan Kimathi, leader of Kenya's Mau Mau Uprising, is captured by a British colonial officer later nicknamed the "Butcher of Bahrain." "I lead them because God never created any nation to be ruled by another nation forever."

WEDNESDAY OCTOBER 18

A Chinese "Boxer," 1900

THURSDAY OCTOBER 19

NOTES:

FRIDAY OCTOBER 20

SATURDAY OCTOBER 21

SUNDAY OCTOBER 22

_____

_____

_____

_____

_____

_____

_____

_____

MONDAY OCTOBER 23

_____

_____

_____

_____

_____

_____

_____

TUESDAY OCTOBER 24

_____

_____

_____

_____

_____

_____

OCTOBER 22, 1964 Jean-Paul Sartre refuses to accept the Nobel Prize for Literature. "The writer must therefore refuse to let himself be transformed into an institution." —LETTER TO THE NOBEL COMMITTEE

OCTOBER 23, 1850 First National Women's Rights Convention meets in Worcester, Massachusetts. The following year, poet and journalist Elizabeth Oakes Smith is nominated as its president, only to be rejected after showing up in a dress baring her neck and arms. "Do we fully understand that we aim at nothing less than an entire subversion of the existing order of society, a dissolution of the whole existing social compact?"

OCTOBER 23, 1856 Du Wenxiu is named Leader of All Muslims in the state established by the Panthay Rebellion, a separatist movement of the Muslim Hui people in southern China. "They scrape from the earth even its skin." —DU WENXIU, WALL POSTER

OCTOBER 27, 1967 The 1967 Abortion Act was passed in the United Kingdom, legalizing abortions for up to 28 weeks. Women in Northern Ireland continue to be excluded from access to this healthcare in their own country.

OCTOBER 28, 1647 The Putney Debates begin, in which members of the New Model Army, who had recently seized London, debate Britain's new constitution. "The poorest man in England is not bound in a strict sense to that government that he hath not had a voice to put himself under." —LEVELLERS SUPPORTER COLONEL RAINSBOROUGH ARGUING FOR UNIVERSAL MALE SUFFRAGE

WEDNESDAY OCTOBER 25

Portrait of Elizabeth Oakes Smith (1806–1893), c. 1845, by John Wesley Paradise

THURSDAY OCTOBER 26

NOTES:

FRIDAY OCTOBER 27

SATURDAY OCTOBER 28

GENTRIFICATION IS INEVITABLE AND OTHER LIES
LESLIE KERN

Gentrifiers are able to weaponize the changes they want to see in "their" neighbourhoods by using the police to address issues such as noise, loitering, games, or other activities they interpret as unpleasant or disorderly. An unhoused person in Toronto's Parkdale neighbourhood told researchers:

> When the Gladstone and the Drake [boutique hotels] finished, that's when everything started happening bad. If I walk this area from nine o'clock in the morning until nine o'clock at night, I can guarantee you, guarantee you without a doubt, I will be stopped at least five times a day. I'm talking handcuffed, searched, put up against the car. Sometimes put under phony arrest, just so that they can throw me in the back of the cop car.

This kind of harassment represents an implicit accord between the police and gentrifiers: by needlessly interfering with people experiencing homelessness, police perform their role as protectors of white middle-classness.

Research has shown that as neighbourhoods gentrify, particularly with white newcomers, calls to 311 (a non-emergency municipal services line) about issues like noise increase substantially. For local bar and restaurant owners, this is more than a nuisance: it often results in fines, harassment of patrons, and threats that they might lose their licences. In New York, the NYPD's "MARCH" project—multi-agency response to community hot spots—is viewed by many as a way of targeting less-desirable businesses and activities in gentrifying neighbourhoods.

Long-time residents are suddenly policed for everything from playing board games on the block to listening to their car stereos. Harlem resident Ramon Hernandez told a Buzzfeed reporter his neighbourly sidewalk domino games were being watched by the police: "It makes me feel bad. I've been living here for more than forty years." Communities targeted by over-policing have long known what gentrification scholars are now beginning to name: that the police act as "shock troops" of gentrification and displacement, enforcing city- and corporate-led development strategies through tactics that lead to the removal of working-class and racialized residents.

In their *People's History of Detroit*, Mark Jay and Philip Conklin argue that the plan to "recapitalize" Detroit uses an explicit law-and-order agenda involving both city police and private security to reassure potential employers that the city is safe. Quicken Loans, the largest mortgage lender in the US, has been at the forefront of this strategy, partnering with police and private security to ensure constant surveillance of the city. This facilitates the further criminalization of poor people and people of colour. Mass incarceration is one way to continue to hollow out inner-city neighbourhoods and prime them for gentrification.

As we well know, calling the police for minor concerns can lead to lethal consequences, especially for people of colour, those with mental illness or disabilities, people experiencing homelessness, and queer and trans people. The murder of Alejandro (Alex) Nieto in March 2014 by police in San Francisco after white newcomers to his Latinx neighbourhood called police while he ate a burrito in a park is just one heartbreaking case of the fatal violence of gentrification. Reporting on the story, Rebecca Solnit noted that the young, white tech workers who considered Nieto suspicious and called 911 mistook his 49ers jacket for gang colours. When the 911 caller's dog went after Nieto's burrito, Nieto reached for his work-issued Taser. Despite being the victim of aggression from the dog, Nieto was killed by police less than five minutes later.

Solnit describes the sentiment of the community that came together to support Nieto's family as the officers eventually went on trial: "Nieto stood for victims of police brutality and for a Latino community that felt imperilled by gentrification, by the wave of evictions and the people who regarded them as menaces and intruders in their own neighbourhood."

In March 2020, Breonna Taylor was murdered by police while sleeping in her home in Louisville, Kentucky, as police implemented a no-knock warrant. In the wake of this egregious killing, lawyers for Taylor's family allege that the raid was part of a "Louisville police department operation to clear out a block in western Louisville that was part of a major gentrification makeover." Their filing argues that the city has been trying to clear certain "holdout" residents from a particular block, including a former boyfriend of Taylor's: "The origin of Breonna's home being raided by police starts with a political need to clear out a street for a large real estate development project."

This is a revised extract from Gentrification is Inevitable and Other Lies *by Leslie Kern (Verso, 2022).*

SUNDAY OCTOBER 29

_____

_____

_____

_____

_____

_____

MONDAY OCTOBER 30

_____

_____

_____

_____

_____

_____

TUESDAY OCTOBER 31

_____

_____

_____

_____

_____

_____

_____

OCTOBER 29, 1888 Li Dazhao, librarian, intellectual, and cofounder of the Chinese Communist Party, is born. "China is a rural nation and most of the laboring class consists of peasants. Unless they are liberated, our whole nation will not be liberated." —"DEVELOP THE PEASANTRY"

OCTOBER 29, 1956 Israel invades Egypt after its nationalization of the Suez Canal, followed a few days later by UK and French troops; they are met with local resistance.

OCTOBER 30, 1969 The Kenya People's Union is banned, transforming the country into a one-party state; its leader, the Luo chief and first vice president of independent Kenya Oginga Odinga, is detained. "We fought for _uhuru_ so that people may rule themselves. Direct action, not underhand diplomacy and silent intrigue by professional politicians, won _uhuru_, and only popular mobilization can make it meaningful." —_NOT YET UHURU_

NOVEMBER 1811 A letter sent from "Ned Ludd" in Nottingham, England, threatens to break the looms of a property owner, in an early document from the Luddite Uprising.

"The guilty may fear but no vengeance he aims
At the honest man's life or Estate"
—LUDDITES, "GENERAL LUDDS TRIUMPH"

NOVEMBER 4, 1780 Quechua leader Túpac Amaru II leads an indigenous rebellion against Spanish control of Peru, beginning with the capture and killing of the Spanish governor by his slave. "There are no accomplices here but you and I. You the oppressor and I the liberator. Both of us deserve to die." —TÚPAC AMARU II, LAST WORDS TO GENERAL JOSÉ ANTONIO DE ARECHE

WEDNESDAY NOVEMBER 1

Chinese comintern Li Dazhao (1888-1927)

THURSDAY NOVEMBER 2

NOTES:

FRIDAY NOVEMBER 3

SATURDAY NOVEMBER 4

SUNDAY NOVEMBER 5

_____

_____

_____

_____

_____

_____

_____

MONDAY NOVEMBER 6

_____

_____

_____

_____

_____

_____

TUESDAY NOVEMBER 7

_____

_____

_____

_____

_____

_____

NOVEMBER 7, 1917 Lenin leads the Bolsheviks in revolution against the provisional Russian government, establishing what will become the Soviet Union. "Freedom in capitalist society always remains about the same as it was in the ancient Greek republics: freedom for the slave-owners."
—THE STATE AND REVOLUTION

NOVEMBER 8, 1775 Thomas Spence, English radical and advocate for common ownership of land, delivers a speech with one of the earliest uses of the term "Rights of Man."

"Ye landlords vile, whose man's place mar,
Come levy rents here if you can;
Your stewards and lawyers I defy,
And live with all the RIGHTS OF MAN"
—"THE REAL RIGHTS OF MAN"

NOVEMBER 8, 1926 Antonio Gramsci, leader of the Italian Communist Party, is arrested by Mussolini and sentenced to twenty years in prison, during which time he would write his famous _Prison Notebooks_. "'Vanguards' without armies to back them up, 'commandos' without infantry or artillery, these too are transpositions from the language of rhetorical heroism." —"VOLUNTARISM AND SOCIAL MASSES"

NOVEMBER 10, 1995 Nigerian government hangs Ken Saro-Wiwa and the rest of the Ogoni Nine for their campaigning against the oil industry, and especially Royal Dutch Shell. "Dance your anger and your joys; dance the military guns to silence; dance their dumb laws to the dump; dance oppression and injustice to death; dance the end of Shell's ecological war of thirty years."
—STATEMENT OF THE OGONI PEOPLE TO THE TENTH SESSION OF THE WORKING GROUP IN INDIGENOUS POPULATIONS

WEDNESDAY NOVEMBER 8

Lenin speaking at an assembly of Red Army troops bound for the Polish front, with Trotsky at the base, Moscow, 1920

THURSDAY NOVEMBER 9

NOTES:

FRIDAY NOVEMBER 10

SATURDAY NOVEMBER 11

SUNDAY NOVEMBER 12

_____

_____

_____

_____

_____

_____

_____

MONDAY NOVEMBER 13

_____

_____

_____

_____

_____

_____

TUESDAY NOVEMBER 14

_____

_____

_____

_____

_____

_____

_____

NOVEMBER 12, 1798 Father of Irish republicanism Wolfe Tone was to be executed by the British for treason, but slit his own throat before the sentence was carried out.

NOVEMBER 13, 1787 Thomas Jefferson, slaveholder and author of the American Declaration of Independence, endorses frequent rebellion in a letter to William Smith. "What signify a few lives lost in a century or two? The tree of liberty must be refreshed from time to time with the blood of patriots and tyrants. It is its natural manure."

NOVEMBER 13, 1792 Louis Antoine de Saint-Just, close friend and ally of Robespierre, delivers his first speech to the revolutionary National Convention in favor of executing the king. "Dare! The word contains all the politics of our revolution."

NOVEMBER 15, 1781 Túpac Katari, Aymara leader of an army that laid siege to the Spanish colonial city of La Paz, Bolivia, is betrayed and killed. "I die but will return tomorrow as thousand thousands." —KATARI'S LAST WORDS

NOVEMBER 15, 1988 Palestinian Declaration of Independence, written by poet Mahmoud Darwish, is proclaimed.

NOVEMBER 16, 1885 Louis Riel, Métis leader who headed two rebellions against a Canadian incursion into their territory, is hanged for treason. "I will perhaps be one day acknowledged as more than a leader of the half-breeds, and if I am I will have an opportunity of being acknowledged as a leader of good in this great country." —RIEL'S FINAL STATEMENT TO THE JURY

WEDNESDAY NOVEMBER 15

The leadership of the PLO during their confrontation with the King of Jordan, 1970

THURSDAY NOVEMBER 16

NOTES:

FRIDAY NOVEMBER 17

SATURDAY NOVEMBER 18

SUNDAY NOVEMBER 19

_____

_____

_____

_____

_____

_____

_____

MONDAY NOVEMBER 20

_____

_____

_____

_____

_____

_____

_____

TUESDAY NOVEMBER 21

_____

_____

_____

_____

_____

_____

_____

NOVEMBER 19, 1915 Joe Hill, militant songwriter and organizer with the International Workers of the World, is executed by firing squad. "Don't waste any time in mourning—organize." —HILL'S FAREWELL LETTER TO BILL HAYWOOD

NOVEMBER 19, 1979 Angela Davis—black feminist, philosopher, and prison abolitionist—wins the vice presidential nomination for the US Communist Party.

NOVEMBER 20, 1969 The Native American group Indians of All Tribes occupies Alcatraz island in the San Francisco Bay and holds it for fourteen months. "Alcatraz Island is more than suitable as an Indian Reservation, as determined by the white man's own standards." —ALCATRAZ PROCLAMATION

NOVEMBER 24, 1947 House Un-American Activities Committee votes to hold the "Hollywood Ten," a group of writers and directors blacklisted for their communist affiliations, in contempt of Congress.

NOVEMBER 24, 2014 A white police officer is acquitted in the shooting death of an unarmed black teenager, Michael Brown, in Ferguson, Missouri, setting off protests nationwide under the moniker Black Lives Matter.

NOVEMBER 25, 1832 Abd al-Qader al-Jaza'iri, Sufi and Muslim scholar and Algerian resistance leader, is elected emir of a confederation of tribes that banded together and fought the French invaders for over a decade.

NOVEMBER 25, 1911 Mexican revolutionary Emiliano Zapata proclaims his Plan de Ayala, laying out his ideology and program of land reform, whose slogan "Land and Freedom!" was a watchword of the Mexican Revolution. "The nation is tired of false men and traitors who make promises like liberators and who on arriving in power forget them and constitute themselves as tyrants."

WEDNESDAY NOVEMBER 22

Angela Davis on her first visit to the Soviet Union, 1972

THURSDAY NOVEMBER 23

NOTES:

FRIDAY NOVEMBER 24

SATURDAY NOVEMBER 25

SUNDAY NOVEMBER 26

_____

_____

_____

_____

_____

_____

_____

MONDAY NOVEMBER 27

_____

_____

_____

_____

_____

_____

_____

TUESDAY NOVEMBER 28

_____

_____

_____

_____

_____

_____

_____

NOVEMBER 29, 1947 The UN approves the partition of Palestine, despite its rejection by Palestinian Arabs and the fact that 90 percent of privately held land was Arab-owned.

> "They've prohibited oppression among them-
>   selves
> but for us they legalized all prohibitions!
> They proclaim, 'Trading with slaves is unlawful'
> but isn't the trading of free people more of
>   a crime?"
> —PALESTINIAN POET ABU SALMA, "MY COUNTRY
> ON PARTITION DAY"

NOVEMBER 30, 1999 The World Trade Organization meeting in Seattle is disrupted by massive anti-globalization protests. "When we smash a window, we aim to destroy the thin veneer of legitimacy that surrounds private property rights." —ACME COLLECTIVE, "ON THE VIOLENCE OF PROPERTY"

DECEMBER 1, 1955 Rosa Parks is arrested for refusing to give up her seat on a segregated bus, which triggers a boycott organized by the Women's Political Council of Montgomery. "Negroes have rights, too, for if Negroes did not ride the busses, they could not operate." —WOMEN'S POLITICAL COUNCIL PAMPHLET

DECEMBER 2, 1964 Berkeley Free Speech Movement leader Mario Savio gives his famous speech on the steps of Sproul Hall. The next day, nearly 800 protesters are arrested on the UC Berkeley campus while resisting restrictions on political speech. "You've got to put your bodies upon the gears and upon the wheels ... upon the levers, upon all the apparatus, and you've got to make it stop."

Rosa Parks (1913–2005) being fingerprinted after her arrest for boycotting public transportation in Montgomery, Alabama, 1956

NOTES:

THE REVOLUTIONARY WOMEN OF EASTERN EUROPE
KRISTEN GHODSEE

To this day, Western feminists dominate the historiography of the global women's movement. Early champions of women's rights like the English Mary Wollstonecraft and John Stuart Mill or the French Olympe de Gouge focused on individual rights. They asserted that since women and men both shared an inherent capacity to reason, differences between the sexes arose from differential socialization rather than from women's supposedly "natural" inferiority. Access to education and the ability to make a living outside of marriage could liberate women from both ignorance and servitude. Later activists like Susan B. Anthony and Elizabeth Cady Stanton in the United States or Emmeline Pankhurst in the United Kingdom built on these ideas to demand women's right to vote. The image of the suffragists animates the popular imagination of what is sometimes referred to as the "first wave" of feminism. In 1979, for example, when the United States Mint issued its first coin featuring the image of an American woman, it chose Susan B. Anthony. In 1999, *Time* magazine named Emmeline Pankhurst as one of the "100 most important people of the 20th century" for her role in winning women the franchise. Later Western feminist icons of the so-called "second wave" include Simone de Beauvoir (author of *The Second Sex*), Betty Friedan (author of *The Feminine Mystique*), and Gloria Steinem (the founder of *Ms. Magazine*). More recently, women like Facebook COO Sheryl Sandberg have carried the torch of Western feminism, admonishing women and girls to "lean in" and break through the remaining barriers that hinder their full equality with men.

But from the earliest days of the development of what we call feminism, there existed an entirely different group of women who, while agreeing that women have the same innate capacity for reason and are therefore deserving of political rights, fought side by side with their male counterparts to create a more equitable world for all. Women in Russia, for example, achieved the franchise in 1917 before most women in the West, and full co-educational access to all universities in Eastern Europe predated that in the United States by decades. Furthermore, women joined the labor force and entered traditionally male professions beginning in the 1920s, and in the 1930s and 1940s, Soviet women were earning doctoral degrees in physics and other natural sciences. A 1957 report of the American Manpower Planning Council noted with some dismay that "there are annually some 13,000 women graduating as engineers in the Soviet Union, compared to well under 100 in the United States." Although they did not have what we in the West would think of as a feminist movement, socialist women enjoyed rapid gains in societies where states made explicit commitments to promote women's economic independence through the radical expansion of social safety nets and special programs to support working mothers.

Despite these achievements, most Western historians and gender scholars have ignored or downplayed the profound importance of socialists for shaping 20th century women's movements. Even the most prominent of these—Alexandra Kollontai, a theorist, teacher, speaker, politician, and diplomat who served as one of the first female ambassadors in the world and was twice nominated for the Nobel Peace Prize—barely gets mentioned in Western textbooks. Her work is completely absent from the 2005 *Feminist Theory: A Philosophical Anthology*, from the 2016 edition of the *Oxford Handbook of Feminist Theory* as well as the 2016 (fourth) and 2021 (fifth) editions of the Routledge *Feminist Theory Reader*. Kollontai's unrelenting antagonism to capitalism apparently undermines her credentials as a "feminist theorist" in liberal circles, even though her ideas and her power to implement them as a politician in the early years of the Soviet Union arguably did more to realize women's full emancipation than the works or deeds of any other woman in the 20th century (including Emmeline Pankhurst!).

This is a revised extract from Red Valkyries: Feminist Lessons from Five Revolutionary Women *by Kristen Ghodsee (Verso, 2022).*

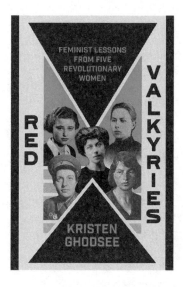

SUNDAY DECEMBER 3

_____

_____

_____

_____

_____

_____

MONDAY DECEMBER 4

_____

_____

_____

_____

_____

_____

TUESDAY DECEMBER 5

_____

_____

_____

_____

_____

_____

_____

DECEMBER 4, 1969 Fred Hampton, Black Panther leader, is assassinated in a raid on his apartment by the Chicago Police with the help of the FBI. "We've got to go up on the mountaintop to make this motherfucker understand, goddamnit, that we are coming from the valley!" —HAMPTON SPEECH AT OLIVET CHURCH

DECEMBER 5, 1978 Wei Jingsheng posts his manifesto "The Fifth Modernization," which was critical of the Communist leadership, to Beijing's Democracy Wall, and is imprisoned for 15 years. "Let us find out for ourselves what should be done."

DECEMBER 6, 1928 The United Fruit Company violently suppresses a workers' strike in Colombia, in what becomes known as the Banana Massacre.

DECEMBER 6, 2008 Greek police shoot and kill Alexandros Grigoropoulos, a fifteen-year-old boy, sparking three weeks of rioting, protests, and occupations around the country. "We are here we are everywhere we are an image from the future." —OCCUPATION STATEMENT, ATHENS SCHOOL OF ECONOMICS AND BUSINESS STUDENTS

DECEMBER 7, 1896 Antonio Maceo, an Afro-Cuban revolutionary, known as the Bronze Titan, dies in the fight for Cuban independence. "Whoever tries to conquer Cuba will gain nothing but the dust of her blood-soaked soil—if he doesn't perish in the struggle first!" —MACEO'S OATH

DECEMBER 9, 2002 To Huu, one of the Viet Minh's most celebrated poets, dies.

"The ditches must go deeper than my hatred. The work must fly faster than my tears." —"GUERILLA WOMAN"

WEDNESDAY DECEMBER 6

Rioters in Athens, 2008

THURSDAY DECEMBER 7

NOTES:

FRIDAY DECEMBER 8

SATURDAY DECEMBER 9

SUNDAY DECEMBER 10

_____

_____

_____

_____

_____

_____

_____

MONDAY DECEMBER 11

_____

_____

_____

_____

_____

_____

_____

TUESDAY DECEMBER 12

_____

_____

_____

_____

_____

_____

DECEMBER 10, 2008 Charter 08, a document for greater democratization, is published, signed by more than 350 Chinese writers, including poet and essayist Woeser, and human rights activist Liu Xiaobo.

DECEMBER 11, 1977 Moroccan poet Saida Menebhi dies in prison after a thirty-four-day hunger strike. Her work was central in the nationwide attempt to recover the history of the thousands of people who were "disappeared" in the 1970s and 1980s.

"Prison is ugly
you draw it my child
with black marks
for the bars and grills"

DECEMBER 11, 2012 Theresa Spence, Chief of Attawapiskat First Nations in Canada, begins a hunger strike that would set off the indigenous sovereignty movement Idle No More.

DECEMBER 13, 1797 Heinrich Heine, German-Jewish poet and essayist, is born. No writer would be more hated by the Nazis.

"Ye fools, so closely to search my trunk!
Ye will find in it really nothing:
My contraband goods I carry about
In my head, not hid in my clothing"
—"A WINTER'S TALE"

DECEMBER 14, 2008 Iraqi journalist Muntadhar al-Zaidi throws his shoe at US president George W. Bush at a press conference. "This is a farewell kiss from the Iraqi people, you dog."

DECEMBER 16, 1656 Radical English Quaker leader James Nayler is arrested for blasphemy after reenacting Christ's entry into Jerusalem by entering Bristol on a donkey.

WEDNESDAY DECEMBER 13

Muntadhar al-Zaidi is pulled away after throwing his shoes at George W. Bush

THURSDAY DECEMBER 14

NOTES:

FRIDAY DECEMBER 15

SATURDAY DECEMBER 16

SUNDAY DECEMBER 17

_____

_____

_____

_____

_____

_____

_____

MONDAY DECEMBER 18

_____

_____

_____

_____

_____

_____

TUESDAY DECEMBER 19

_____

_____

_____

_____

_____

_____

_____

DECEMBER 18, 2010 Demonstrations begin in Tunisia, the day after street vendor Mohammed Bouazizi self-immolated in protest of harassment from officials, setting off what would eventually become the Arab Spring.

DECEMBER 19, 1944 US soldier Kurt Vonnegut becomes a Nazi prisoner of war. The experience later shapes his novels, which often explore anti-authoritarian and anti-war themes. "There is no reason goodness cannot triumph over evil, so long as the angels are as organized as the Mafia." —*CAT'S CRADLE*

DECEMBER 20, 1986 More than 30,000 students march through Shanghai chanting pro-democracy slogans. "When will the people be in charge?"

DECEMBER 23, 1970 After being captured in Bolivia while working as a chronicler for Che Guevara, French journalist Régis Debray is released from prison. "For Che the true difference, the true frontier, is not the one which separates a Bolivian from a Peruvian, a Peruvian from an Argentinian, an Argentinian from a Cuban. It is the one that separates the Latin Americans from the Yankees." —DEBRAY'S TESTIMONY AT HIS COURT-MARTIAL

DECEMBER 23, 1986 Dissident and Nobel Peace Prize–winner Andrei Sakharov returns to Moscow after six years spent in internal exile for protesting the Soviet war in Afghanistan. "Freedom of thought is the only guarantee against an infection of people by mass myths, which, in the hands of treacherous hypocrites and demagogues, can be transformed into bloody dictatorship."

WEDNESDAY DECEMBER 20

_____

_____

_____

_____

_____

_____

_____

Demonstrators face police lines on Aveunue Bourguiba, Central Tunis, 2011

THURSDAY DECEMBER 21

_____

_____

_____

_____

_____

_____

_____

NOTES:

_____

_____

_____

_____

_____

_____

FRIDAY DECEMBER 22

_____

_____

_____

_____

_____

_____

_____

SATURDAY DECEMBER 23

_____

_____

_____

_____

_____

_____

_____

SUNDAY DECEMBER 24

_____

_____

_____

_____

_____

_____

_____

_____

MONDAY DECEMBER 25

_____

_____

_____

_____

_____

_____

_____

TUESDAY DECEMBER 26

_____

_____

_____

_____

_____

_____

_____

DECEMBER 25, 1831 Samuel Sharpe, leader of the Native Baptists of Montego Bay, leads Jamaican slaves in the Great Jamaican Slave Revolt, which was instrumental in abolishing chattel slavery. "I would rather die upon yonder gallows than live in slavery." —SHARPE'S LAST WORDS

DECEMBER 25, 1927 B. R. Ambedkar, an architect of the Indian constitution who was born into the Dalit caste of "untouchables," leads followers to burn the Manusmriti, an ancient text justifying the hierarchy. The "untouchables" were relegated to occupations considered impure, like butchering and waste removal.

DECEMBER 25, 1977 Domitila Barrios de Chungara, an activist with the militant Bolivian labor group Housewives' Committee, begins a hunger strike that leads to the end of the US-backed Bolivian dictatorship. "The first battle to be won is to let the woman, the man, the children participate in the struggle of the working class, so that the home can become a stronghold that the enemy can't overcome."

DECEMBER 30, 1884 William Morris, Eleanor Marx, and others establish the Socialist League, a revolutionary organization in the UK. "Civilization has reduced the workman to such a skinny and pitiful existence, that he scarcely knows how to frame a desire for any life much better." —MORRIS, "HOW I BECAME A SOCIALIST"

DECEMBER 30, 1896 José Rizal, Filipino nationalist revolutionary and writer, is executed by the Spanish on charges of rebellion, sedition, and conspiracy.

WEDNESDAY DECEMBER 27

B. R. Ambedkar during his tenure as chairman of the committee for drafting the constitution, 1950

THURSDAY DECEMBER 28

NOTES:

FRIDAY DECEMBER 29

SATURDAY DECEMBER 30

SUNDAY DECEMBER 31

_____

_____

_____

_____

_____

_____

_____

MONDAY JANUARY 1 2024

_____

_____

_____

_____

_____

_____

_____

TUESDAY JANUARY 2 2024

_____

_____

_____

_____

_____

_____

_____

DECEMBER 31, 1977 Kenyan writer Ngũgĩ wa Thiong'o is imprisoned for cowriting a play critical of the Kenyan government.

> "We the workers in factories and plantations said in one voice:
> We reject slave wages!
> Do you remember the 1948 general strike?"
> —NGŨGĨ WA THIONG'O AND NGŨGĨ WA MIRII, _I WILL MARRY WHEN I WANT_

JANUARY 1, 1970 Gil Scott-Heron, the poet and recording artist who became a voice of black protest culture, releases his album _Small Talk at 125th and Lenox_, whose opening track is, "The Revolution Will Not be Televised."

> "The revolution will not make you look five pounds thinner,
> the revolution will not be televised, Brother."

JANUARY 3, 1961 Angolan peasants employed by the Portuguese-Belgium cotton plantation company Cotonang begin protests over poor working conditions, setting off the Angolan struggle for independence from Portugal.

> "Tomorrow we will sing songs of freedom when we commemorate
> the day this slavery ends."
> —FIRST PRESIDENT OF ANGOLA AND LEADER OF THE MOVEMENT FOR THE LIBERATION OF ANGOLA ANTONIO AGOSTINHO NETO, "FAREWELL AT THE HOUR OF PARTING"

JANUARY 6, 1977 Charter 77, a document criticizing the Czech government for its human rights record, is published; it is violently suppressed.

WEDNESDAY JANUARY 3 2024

Gil Scott-Heron (1949–2011)

THURSDAY JANUARY 4 2024

NOTES:

FRIDAY JANUARY 5 2024

SATURDAY JANUARY 6 2024

V

VERSO READING LISTS

RADICAL HISTORIES

INSURGENT EMPIRE: ANTICOLONIALISM AND THE MAKING OF BRITISH DISSENT
PRIYAMVADA GOPAL

THE COMMON WIND: AFRO-AMERICAN CURRENTS IN THE AGE OF THE HAITIAN REVOLUTION
JULIUS S SCOTT.

SET THE NIGHT ON FIRE: L.A. IN THE SIXTIES
MIKE DAVIS AND JON WIENER

DARING TO HOPE: MY LIFE IN THE 1970S
SHEILA ROWBOTHAM

OCTOBER: THE STORY OF THE RUSSIAN REVOLUTION
CHINA MIÉVILLE

THE AMERICAN CRUCIBLE: SLAVERY, EMANCIPATION AND HUMAN RIGHTS
ROBIN BLACKBURN

LINEAGES OF THE ABSOLUTIST STATE
PERRY ANDERSON

ECOLOGY AND CLIMATE CHANGE

HOW TO BLOW UP A PIPELINE: LEARNING TO FIGHT IN A WORLD ON FIRE
ANDREAS MALM

THE CASE FOR THE GREEN NEW DEAL
ANN PETTIFOR

A PLANET TO WIN: WHY WE NEED A GREEN NEW DEAL
KATE ARONOFF, ALYSSA BATTISTONI, ET AL.

THE CLIMATE CRISIS AND THE GLOBAL GREEN NEW DEAL: THE POLITICAL ECONOMY OF SAVING THE PLANET
NOAM CHOMSKY AND ROBERT POLLIN

PLANET ON FIRE: A MANIFESTO FOR THE AGE OF ENVIRONMENTAL BREAKDOWN
MATHEW LAWRENCE AND LAURIE LAYBOURN-LANGTON

FOSSIL CAPITAL: THE RISE OF STEAM POWER AND THE ROOTS OF GLOBAL WARMING
ANDREAS MALM

WORK AND AUTOMATION

WORK WITHOUT THE WORKER: LABOUR IN THE AGE OF PLATFORM CAPITALISM
PHIL JONES

AUTOMATION AND THE FUTURE OF WORK
AARON BENANAV

OVERTIME: WHY WE NEED A SHORTER WORKING WEEK
KYLE LEWIS AND WILL STRONG

WHY YOU SHOULD BE A TRADE UNIONIST
LEN McCLUSKEY

FULLY AUTOMATED LUXURY COMMUNISM: A MANIFESTO
AARON BASTANI

FEMINISM AND GENDER

THE VERSO BOOK OF FEMINISM:
REVOLUTIONARY WORDS FROM FOUR
MILLENNIA OF REBELLION
EDITED BY JESSIE KINDIG

GLITCH FEMINISM
LEGACY RUSSELL

ABOLISH THE FAMILY:
A MANIFESTO FOR CARE AND LIBERATION
SOPHIE LEWIS

FEMINISM FOR THE 99%: A MANIFESTO
CINZIA ARRUZZA, TITHI BHATTACHARYA AND
NANCY FRASER

BURN IT DOWN!
FEMINIST MANIFESTOS FOR THE REVOLUTION
EDITED BY BREANNE FAHS

REVOLTING PROSTITUTES:
THE FIGHT FOR SEX-WORKERS' RIGHTS
MOLLY SMITH AND JUNO MAC

FEMINISM AND NATIONALISM
IN THE THIRD WORLD
KUMARI JAYAWARDENA

ECONOMICS

THE NEW SPIRIT OF CAPITALISM
LUC BOLTANSKI AND EVE CHIAPELLO

THE PRODUCTION OF MONEY:
HOW TO BREAK THE POWER OF BANKERS
ANN PETTIFOR

THE COMPLETE WORKS OF ROSA LUXEMBURG,
VOLUME II: ECONOMIC WRITINGS 2
ROSA LUXEMBURG

A COMPANION TO MARX'S CAPITAL,
VOLUME 1 AND VOLUME 2
DAVID HARVEY

FORTUNES OF FEMINISM: FROM STATE-
MANAGED CAPITALISM TO NEOLIBERAL CRISIS
NANCY FRASER

RACE AND ETHNICITY

FUTURES OF BLACK RADICALISM
EDITED BY GAYE THERESA JOHNSON
AND ALEX LUBIN

A KICK IN THE BELLY:
WOMEN, SLAVERY AND RESISTANCE
STELLA DADZIE

IF THEY COME IN THE MORNING ... :
VOICES OF RESISTANCE
EDITED BY ANGELA Y. DAVIS

RACECRAFT:
THE SOUL OF INEQUALITY
IN AMERICAN LIFE
KAREN E. FIELDS AND BARBARA J. FIELDS

HOW EUROPE UNDERDEVELOPED AFRICA
WALTER RODNEY

BEYOND BLACK AND WHITE:
FROM CIVIL RIGHTS TO BARACK OBAMA
MANNING MARABLE

ACTIVISM AND RESISTANCE

THE VERSO BOOK OF DISSENT:
REVOLUTIONARY WORDS FROM THREE
MILLENNIA OF REBELLION AND RESISTANCE
EDITED BY ANDREW HSIAO AND AUDREA LIM

THE END OF POLICING
ALEX S. VITALE

OUR HISTORY IS THE FUTURE:
STANDING ROCK VERSUS THE DAKOTA
ACCESS PIPELINE, AND THE LONG TRADITION
OF INDIGENOUS RESISTANCE
NICK ESTES

DIRECT ACTION:
PROTEST AND THE REINVENTION
OF AMERICAN RADICALISM
L.A. KAUFFMAN

ABOLITION GEOGRAPHY:
ESSAYS TOWARDS LIBERATION
RUTH WILSON GILMORE

POLITICAL THEORY

DECOLONIAL MARXISM:
ESSAYS FROM THE PAN-AFRICAN REVOLUTION
WALTER RODNEY

HOW TO BE AN ANTICAPITALIST
IN THE TWENTY-FIRST CENTURY
ERIK OLIN WRIGHT

THE ORIGIN OF CAPITALISM
A LONGER VIEW
ELLEN MEISKINS WOOD

IMAGINED COMMUNITIES: REFLECTIONS ON THE
ORIGIN AND SPREAD OF NATIONALISM
BENEDICT ANDERSON

FOR A LEFT POPULISM
CHANTAL MOUFFE

ART AND AESTHETICS

ARTIFICIAL HELLS: PARTICIPATORY ART
AND THE POLITICS OF SPECTATORSHIP
CLAIRE BISHOP

CULTURE STRIKE:
ART AND MUSEUMS IN AN AGE OF PROTEST
LAURA RAICOVICH

ALL THAT IS SOLID MELTS INTO AIR:
THE EXPERIENCE OF MODERNITY
MARSHALL BERMAN

PORTRAITS: JOHN BERGER ON ARTISTS
JOHN BERGER

AISTHESIS: SCENES FROM
THE AESTHETIC REGIME OF ART
JACQUES RANCIÈRE

CITIES AND ARCHITECTURE

FEMINIST CITY:
CLAIMING SPACE IN A MAN-MADE WORLD
LESLIE KERN

MUNICIPAL DREAMS:
THE RISE AND FALL OF COUNCIL HOUSING
JOHN BOUGHTON

EXTRASTATECRAFT:
THE POWER OF INFASTRUCTURE SPACE
KELLER EASTERLING

CAPITAL CITY:
GENTRIFICATION AND THE REAL ESTATE STATE
SAMUEL STEIN

REBEL CITIES: FROM THE RIGHT TO THE CITY
TO THE URBAN REVOLUTION
DAVID HARVEY

PHILOSOPHY AND THEORY

THE FORCE OF NONVIOLENCE:
THE ETHICAL IN THE POLITICAL
JUDITH BUTLER

THE LEFT HEMISPHERE:
MAPPING CRITICAL THEORY TODAY
RAZMIG KEUCHEYAN

CRITIQUE OF EVERYDAY LIFE
HENRI LEFEBVRE

MINIMA MORALIA:
REFLECTIONS FROM DAMAGED LIFE
THEODOR ADORNO

NO WALLS, NO BORDERS

THE DISPOSSESSED: A STORY OF ASYLUM
AT THE US–MEXICAN BORDER AND BEYOND
JOHN WASHINGTON

AGAINST BORDERS: THE CASE FOR ABOLITION
GRACIE MAE BRADLEY AND LUKE DE NORONHA

ALL-AMERICAN NATIVISM:
HOW THE BIPARTISAN WAR ON IMMIGRANTS
EXPLAINS POLITICS AS WE KNOW IT
DANIEL DENVIR

WE BUILT THE WALL:
HOW THE US KEEPS OUT ASYLUM SEEKERS FROM
MEXICO, CENTRAL AMERICA AND BEYOND
EILEEN TRUAX

VIOLENT BORDERS:
REFUGEES AND THE RIGHT TO MOVE
REECE JONES

NOTES

NOTES